TIMELESS ECHOES

(Moral and Historical Philosophies)

Volume 2

By Ekundayo Oruamen

PREFACE

This second volume is explosive in contents.

The world body, United Nations, is humbly urged to take a special note of the role assigned to it. It has the responsibility to save the future world.

Timeless Echoes is a book not only for reading pleasure but for the big message delivered in several subtitles.

Ekundayo Oruamen

APPRECIATION

A tribute to my late brother, Pa Isaac U. Oruamen. He laid the foundation of this book. I only built on it, in the sense he gave me the little education I needed to do this.

Appreciation to all my male children for their helps in various ways. Especially to Pharm. Stephen Omooje and Peter Abiodun Omolei who supplied the needed information and posted adverts on the internet, I being too old to move around and illiterate in the modern world of social media platform. To whom also I left the responsibility of publishing.

Time-worn "wise" sayings are done in quotes; otherwise all the sayings are original. I do not dwell on lengthy monologue but the essence and the lessons from the subject matter.

In the presentations attempts are made to correct our wayward behaviours, nurture the mind, and mould the conscience and the reformation of characters.

Moral advices and historical illustrations on position, freedom and power I spoke much about are to educate the holders of these intoxicating qualities to beware of the way they make use of them to avoid possible downfall. This is why the historical illustrations feature mostly in volume 2.

The book is aimed to set us on the right path of peace and brotherly co-existence, serves as a beacon to lighten the tortuous way on our journey in life. It reveals strong indices which convincingly are threats to man's continuous existence on planet Earth, else extinction of all organic lives. Not assumption but based on fact.

Timeless Echoes is a basket of wisdom!

Timeless Echoes will continue to re-echo from generation to generation as best words on marble.

CONTENT

1091. Broadway Of Knowledge.
1092. Survival.
1093. Survival Instincts
1094. Rubbished By Civilization
1095. No End In Sight
1096. Unless The Taproot
1097. A Flaming Sword.
1098. Made To Suffer Ignominious Death
1099. A Million Years Ahead
1100. Nature's Unpredictabilities
1101. Self Preservation From Danger
1102. President Without Sceptre
1103. A Political Arena
1104. Divine Intervention
1105. The Three Pillars
1106. Kissing Culture
1107. No Organic Creature
1108. Voluntary Resignation
1109. In My Grandfather's Compound
1110. Wandering Mind
1111. Risk In Trust
1112. Your Rights
1113. Existence !
1114. Election Blue.
1115. Just The State Of Mind
1116. The Big Rivers
1117. Corruption Witch
1118. No Devil Without Man
1119. Evil Agents.
1120. Spilled Milk
1121. Language Extinction
1122. I Will Fly
1123. Common Property
1124. "Before Abraham Was.....

1159. Seamless Handover
1160. The Gallant Soldier
1161. Unitary Structure,
1162. The Doyen Of Journalism
1163. Deluded People
1164. Under Table Political Chess Game
1165. A Crack On The Wall
1166. Died On The "Throne"
1167. Rose From Grass To Grace,
1168. Penkele Mess,
1169. And The Spirit Of God
1170. The Only Institution
1171. Politicians Have No Conscience
1172. Making Mistakes
1173. Only The Poor
1174. On The Knoll
1175. The Devil's Dining Table.
1176. Categories Of Politics
1177. When Congo Boiled
1178. Status Of A Country.
1179. Dearth Of Leadership.
1180. Born To Die,
1181. Pushed By The Devil
1182. Two Decades Of History,
1181. The Shade Of Wickedness
1184. Used As Chips
1185. Who Is Minister For Corruption?
1186. The Pathway Of Evolution
1187. Struggle Between Good And Evil
1188. Quarrel
1189. Day And Night
1190. The Glorious Days
1191. Deaf To Advice
1192. We All Have A Religion

TIMELESS ECHOES

(Moral and Historical Philosophies)

VOL. TWO

901. “This Is Nigeria”

Where anything goes” Is a common expression
By her citizens where things do not work
As they should because they are not done
In the proper manner.
This is a sad commentary for a country

That wishes to peer with other progressive ones
And also wishes to be respected.
We are still searching for dedicated patriots
To put her on the right course to progress.

902. Like Sweet Dreams

Which come to reality is the case
Of some men who may not have made it
A success though tried or not.
But luck hooks them onto successful women,
To become men of means sounds like some
Sweet dreams.
Such men should not regard themselves belittled
Or feel ashamed;
It is one of the throw – up jokes of life.

903. Africa Must Wake Up

And rise from its deep slumber and come of age,
Especially the black, who still play the dumb
And naivety.
We continue to subject ourselves to second class citizens
And allow ourselves be treated as dimwits
When we have the wherewithal to make it great.
Instead we ignore all the wealth in our backyard
And look up to the whites for financial
Donors for all our needs.
Even for common things we can make here
Because we fail to seriously look inward.
It is our self-seeking rulers who parade themselves
As progressive democrats that had led us
Into this unproductive impasse.

904. Inferior Mentality

Exhibits by the high and the mighty in underdeveloped

Countries has become ego boosting and social pride.
They want to be seen being flown to Whiteman's land
Even for common headache,
While they intentionally neglect their own health sector.
They go abroad as VIPs in flying coffins
And come back as packed sardine.

905. Leading A Fast Life

On a fast lane will surely end in crash unexpectedly
Like over speeding vehicle on an uneven road.
Unless you reconsider and quickly reverse
Your life style in the nick of time.

906. Your neighbours

Are your immediate brothers and sisters
That will rally round you in time of crises
Before your distant blood relatives.
Therefore it is foolishness for somebody to claim
To have nothing to do with his or her
Immediate neighbours.

907. The African Child

Has delayed physical growth,
Insufficient early grasp of speech and intelligence
Unlike his counterpart in Europe and America, etc.
Perhaps the delayed development of the continent generally
Is an off-shoot from the delay of the African child.

908. Fiction Writers

Are special breed given unequal talent to create
Non-existent epics of wonderful genre.
I doff my hat for them and say well-done
To endowed genius of imaginative creativity:

They are indeed a unique set of people

909. Militancy

Has suddenly become a new lucrative profession
As an easy avenue to earn sweat free money
In the guise of fighting for the general interest
Of the common people and the whole community.
It has created overnight kingpins whose activities
Do not benefit anybody but themselves alone.

910. Retaining The Loyalty

Of your servant for maximum obedience is very instructive
Instead of exercising maximum and coercive authority
Which may be counter productive.
It pays to accord your servant or paid worker
Some level of respect and a little reward
Once in awhile to retain his or her absolute loyalty.
The move is likely to ensure personal safety
And productivity.

911. Advantage Of United Majority

Proves the saying: "Minority will have their say
The majority their way".
The majority will always win against the minority
To prove the reality of the game of number
And the truism in Hitler's Germany against
The united majority of the Allied countries.

912. Yuletide Madness

When almost everybody falls a victim of its lure
Of feverish season and lose all sense of reason
And humane disposition,
The season we cause our neighbours all manner
Of inconveniences and sorrow to satisfy ourselves.

Yet we are supposed to be celebrating
The Yuletide of our Lord for His humility
And the goodness He gave the world.

913. It Is A False Claim

When politicians win elections through rigging
And claim victory to God's doing.
They are only ashamed to owe victory
To their godfather the devil.
Is it not why they do not fear God
When cheating their people?

914. Why Politicians Get Away

With everything is because the problem with our people
Is they ruled by their greedy nature
And sway by their stomach.
The politicians cash in on these weaknesses
To deceive them
Because they are not controlled by their heads.

915. Negative Sensitivity To Criticism

Is the bane of an average black man.
He has no thick-skinned quality to absorb
Constructive criticism,
Especially from his superiors with better arguments.
He displays peevish defiance and becomes sarcastic
To better judgment.
Which is why he fails to follow progressive path.

916. To Pass Exams

First read all questions from one to last number.
Begin to answer those you feel are easy
To tackle before the difficult ones.
In this way you will save time to answer

The easy ones before getting to the ones
Hard to solve.
If you begin with difficult questions you may discover
To your dismay that you have devoted
All the allotted time cracking them and no
More time left for the ones you are likely
To do well.
This advice applies to all problems you are involved in.
The best and easy way of approach.

917. Political Naivety

He who observes strictly all the moral principles
Guiding electoral rules is politically naive
And is not ready to win elections in a country.
Where winning elections free and fair is alien
He will have to wait until,
Only God knows when,
The emancipation of people's minds politically.

918. As Nature Orders It

Human being will behave as human being,
And animal like animal.
So nature had made all creatures in that order,
And nature itself is the best judge of character.

919. As Nature Demands

Human beings build homes,
Some animals burrow into the ground
While the wild ones seek for their lair
And birds build nests on tree branches
And under the leaves.
All in a bid to shelter themselves from
The fury of the hostile elements,
All manner of harmful denizens prowling the earth

And to seek rest in comfort.

920. Business Technique

All successful businesses have their initial ups
And downs of difficulties.
With patience and forbearance a light must appear
At the end of the tunnel that will usher in
Hope and crowning success.
Your guiding rule is risk management technique.

921. When Not To Be Annoyed

When somebody is trying to provoke you
By words or action refrain from ventilating
Your spleen but calmly explain your own points
Unless the person persists on having his or her
Own way against your opinion.
Still display calm determination in response without
Trace of annoyance and "going off the hook".
With this calm attitude people will respect your views.

922. Dual Spirits

In man as embodiment of good and evil minds,
Has freedom of choice between the two spirits.
Either of the dual spirits he submits himself
To control his actions depends on the level
Of his willpower,
Which is also influenced by both internal and
External forces.
Everything boils down to what extent can individual
Control his or her willpower.

923. Too Much Of Rhetoric

Produce little or no meaningful action and result.
All the intended actions dissolve in too much talk

Like smoke dissolving into the air.

924. **In God's Own Plan**

For you must play your own part in it.
God will not promise one thing and do another
Unless you fail to do your own part.

925. **Africa The Land Of Sunshine**

Is the most fortunate among the rest of the continents
Which is not ravaged by natural disasters
But by its ruling crop of leaders.
Which proves true the saying of our people,
"He who has head has no cap
One with a cap has no head".

926. **Loss Of Essence**

The white man cannot come to my fatherland,
Colonize me and confiscate my fatherland
And also erodes my traditions and customs.
A people colonized by white man and allowed
Their traditions and customs to be eroded and buried
Have lost the essence of meaningful existence.

927. **Our Modern Prison**

We have become prisoners in our own homes,
Thanks to the marauding bad boys and girls.
The irony of it is that we are now so deluded
We have come to regard our modern prison cage
With pride and a mark of status symbol.

928. **Destroying Their Own Economy**

To build the economies of other lands.
Authorities in advanced societies build infrastructures
For the wellbeing of their upcoming generations

So themselves can live in comfort.
But in our own clime those in charge
Of our commonwealth misappropriate and embezzle
Money meant for building infrastructures,
Buy for themselves mansions and exotic cars.
The excesses they lodge in banks abroad,
Acquire businesses and properties in foreign lands
To develop their already developed economies.

929. Organ Of Secrecy

In government is run by three portfolio holders:
Spokesperson to the President is the chief
Lying mouth organ,
His media aide is the chief propagandist
And the Minister of information the chief liar
For the government.
All combine to keep members of the public
Behind the wall of government activities.

930. Governance By Rhetoric

When the politicians have won elections
Either through the front or back door,
All you see is a lot of political motions
But no movement at governance.
After the first two years of abracadabra
The rest is devoted to a lot of political rhetoric
And political shenanigans

931. Minority And Majority

Having their say and the other their way round
Is a popular saying all over.
But here the scenario plays out upside down:
The majority have their say the few minority
Overlords in power have their way.

If the majority chose to remain in docility
The mediocre leaders will always have their way.

932. "Robbing Peter To Pay Paul"

Too many people in the society this modern day,
Although few in number
Compared with the country's census figures,
Are earning too much basic salaries and allowances.
Yet without commensurate workload to the detriment
Of the hardworking masses.
If this set of "robbing Peter to pay Paul" categories
Are by any providence robbed in any form
They do not deserve the people's sympathy
Whom they are indirectly robbing as allowed
By a faulty system.
They only shed some of their excess baggage.

933. Letter V As National Identity

Every country has a particular identification tag
Attached to its national life.
One of such countries is the former
Union of Soviet Socialist Republics whose identity
Is sharply reflected in their names.
Anyone from the republics who does not
Have letter v in any of his or her names
May not be regarded a true native of the land.

934. They Ruled The Waves

At a period the might of a nation
Was the capability to navigate the mighty seas.
At a time they won wars on the high seas
And land,
Whose kings must lead wars with a show
O f naked power.

A nation that defeated the great Spanish Armada
And other swashbuckling feats,
Which earned them the noble appellation of
The Great Britain!
A great empire which ruled many countries as colonies,
Even North America as New England.

935. The Highest Species

And the most intelligent on Earth is man,
Equipped with all it takes to make his world
A paradise for himself.
But what does he do with the intellectual
Potentialities he is so gifted with but also
To his disadvantage by turning the world
Into a theatre of horror and making his life
Also a tortuous journey.

936. Worshipping Tribal Heritage

Hardly anyone who does not bow before tribal shrine
No matter his or her nationalistic philosophies.
Tribal instincts take precedence over national
Aspiration.
It is instinctively natural to bend to tribal sentiments.

937. But For God's Intervention

The people are always left afloat in misery
By their leaders.
In a humane society government knows
Its obligations
To the people and discharge them accordingly.
In my own country government equally knows
Its obligations but will not honour them.
So the people seek for God's divine interventions

To enter into the hearts of their leaders
To do the needful.

938. Plucking Money On Tree

Would have been a rare feat to accomplish
Unlike plucking fruits.
If you find money to be earned the easy way
You got to be very careful and be wary
Because no easy way to getting money.
Were it possible to pluck money on trees
Like fruits
The trees will be so tall and smooth
On the body without low branches
For easy climbing.

939. The Mark Of Free Thinker

Not tainted by any creed and ruled
By mundane and religious ideologies.
A free and liberal minded is the mark
of an unbiased thinker.

940. State Sponsored Assassin

Is not caught because the crime is planned
And executed by the top hierarchy of government.
But you must know that when you commit
Heinous and clandestine crime on behalf
of the state you may be sacrificing your own life
For the cause.
The state will not want a living witness
Outside its enclave.

941. A Slip of Tongue

Or a misquote if I heard aright that
The oga at the top said there was much money

In government purse but how to spend it?
And this happened in a country where infrastructures
Are lacking and the few available are in
Various states of decay.
He can be forgiven for his youthful inexperience.
After all despite presiding over enormous resources
From oil he did not enrich himself,
From which his successors became emperors
Overnight and built empires for themselves,
But did nothing to improve on his legacy.

942. Blessed Rain

That falls for the sake of the downtrodden people,
For anytime it rains give them the opportunity
To enjoy respite from the extensive heat
Since they could not afford the price of generators
Or fuel to power them.
The people get relief from collecting rain water
Under the eaves of their roofs,
For there is no government to care.

943. Definition of God:

Nobody knows what air,
Wind or breeze is like.
But we know about it through breathing it,
And the particles it carries in its action.
Therefore nobody knows what God is like,
We only know about Him through His creation.
Whatever power or force that created the Universe
And sustain it is called God.
Non physical but a Spiritual Enigma!

944. Philosophy of Belonging

To everybody and to nobody

Yet showing clear cases of nepotism in its true colour.
It is in line with our rulers to say
One thing and do the opposite,
All in the name of democratic practices
We love to Christine learning process.

945. Too Self-centred

He has the heart of a lion
And the courage of a warrior,
But the spirit of selfish ego.
He has all it takes to move his country
To the pinnacle of her glory
While at the helm of affairs.
But all was sacrificed for personal ego
To be the cynosure of the entire world.

946. My Fine Clothe

I once admired so much and appreciated
By people but now used to taters,
Discarded and put away as a rag.
If you have read my views on death
And burial of the material body
Then you know my mind.

947. Can Of Worms

is often opened to reveal colossal thefts
In the system through dubious methods,
And of other anti social crimes.
Corruption floods are immediately released
to wash away the embarrassing worms.

948. Bad Rule

Is not often the fault of the so – called leaders

But the people who in their complacency
Allowed themselves to be led as a flock of sheep
Away from the green pasture to the arid land.

949. Be Humble

Before the people under your control;
That will chance your power of authority over them.
In that way they will willingly respect
And obey your orders.

950. The Chess Of Fate

Being played by everybody takes place
On the chessboard of the world.
Let everybody play his or her own role
As thinks best.
If good you win good fortune,
If bad you
earn bad reward.
Nothing is lost on the chessboard of Fate!

951. Made A Fool Of

By every successive government as they all
Have ready cock and bull stories to keep
The allegiance of the citizens.
They all have three things in common:
Urge the people to bear with them,
Make sacrifices and tighten their belts
While in the meantime they loosen theirs
So their stomach can take in more.

952. Business Sagacity

Is needed in the transactions of your business
If you want to make profit;
But must be fair in your business deal.

If you want to be the good man
Of the people in running your business
They will plunge you into liquidation
Before you know it.

953. A Fool By Choice

If anybody is pretending ignorance as excuse
To criticize his neighbor, is a bigger fool.
A confirmed fool is better than him.

954. Wearing Beard

Is exclusive ornament dignifying the status
of the aged,
More so when it has turned grayish bushy.

955. Nothing Is Absolutely 100% Balance

No matter how bad a man is he must have
Some iota of good in his makeup.
Likewise as good a man can be he must
Have some few characteristic inadequacies,
Because nobody is completely whole.

956. Knowledge Of God

By all people did not originate from the Bible.
The Bible confirms this by acknowledging
That the Gentiles worshipped strange gods.
Religion originated from traditions and customs
As a set of rules and orders to follow,
And acknowledgement of God or gods depends
On the level of awareness by individual
Set of people through their traditions and customs.
God is the unifying Force in the universal
Chain in His creation.

957. You Are On Your Own

If you are poor and depend on government
In this part of the world to solve your problem.
Unless you find a way to circumvent it.
Either offer a bribe or know a member
Or the inner circle.

958. Lucky Or Unlucky

Not to have been awarded a gold medal
For unofficially legalizing graft?
He won them over with his gap tooted smiles
And made bribe inducement an official transaction
Of government business.
His successors gradually improve on it.

If you are in agreement.

Anyone who could read between the lines knew this.

959. National Grid A Sour Taste

I suppose you've watched our teenage girls
Playing game of throwing forward small pebbles or
Stones in a square drawn on the ground
With other small squares within and balancing on
One leg hop after the throw.
If you are not an expert balancing on one
Leg you fall.
This is what is playing out at Nigeria's National electricity grid.
While the girls are experts balancing and hopping
On one leg
The national grid is an exponent balancing on one
Wobbling leg staggering and collapsing every now and again.

960. Crocodile Tears

Are shed by our so-called leaders to show sympathies
How much they love and care for victims of misfortunes.
It is all charade and false tears
For the benefit of the general public.
In most cases they are handy with handkerchiefs
Sprinkled with chemical substances that sting the eyes
To draw tears.

961. Superpower Nations Dirty Hands

of meddlesome manoeuvre and intrigue
in the murky water of underdeveloped countries
of the third world's politics.
These meddlesome interlopers are invariably cabal
From the super power nations who must have
Their fingers in political juicy pie of these
Underdeveloped countries.
They have their Judases as stooges in these countries
To help throw spanner in the works if the leaders
Are so foolish and prove stubborn to promote
Their economic interest.
Their chief aim is to topple such governments
And install their surrogate puppets through whom
They can control their economies.

962. International Diplomacy

Is a political game of intrigue played in
International arena by the advanced countries
To woo and win over the less developed ones.
Their promises of juicy aid in both monetary
And infrastructural development
With backup glowing speeches
Are just rhetoric but hollow and watering
Because the promises even when kept are indirectly
Taken back with interest through the backdoor.

963. Nobody Controls Life

Without some hitches along the line.
While some try to choose the straight road
To righteousness and miss it some are fortunate,
Many others chose the crooked road to crime.
In our individual choice of good or evil
Impartial justice,
The final arbiter of human behaviours
Will intervene to serve everyone of us
The due deserts we deserve.

964. Stand Up For Light

Even if the power of witchcraft is controlled
By evil spirits,
For good sometimes comes out of evil.
The cult of witchcraft can be turned into
A noble art for good purposes and be thrown
Open into limelight as acceptable religion
For the advancement of human dignity
And for the advancement of human race.
The practitioners are shortchanging themselves
By refusing to reborn into the modern theatre
Of enlightenment through religion and science.
Be amalgamated into a body of intellectual
Members of wizards,
Witches and other related allies by turning
The practice into an acclaimed modern religion
of light worldwide.]

965. Like Hazy Pictures

Nothing can really be clearly defined
While in the state of dreaming.
Because you do not really control the interplay

Of action.
Nothing solidly tangible to hold onto
Wherever you are or whatever
you are doing
You do not actually belong.
Which is why some come into clear recollection,
Some scantly or nothing

966. Not A Pride

That our graduates should be reduced to doing
Menial jobs because standard of education
Has fallen low in the land or because
The jobs are not just there;
Or because the graduates are half baked products
It is a national embarrassment for which
We all should cover our face in shame
To have come to this sorrow state.
So far our generation has failed the youths
In the land.

967. Human Capital Development

Is very germane to any country's progress.
If this critical aspect of running a country
Is missing those so-called leaders in charge
Are deliberately crucifying and mortgaging
The future of such country,
And mine falls squarely into this category.
Two major factors responsible for the impasse
In developing our human capital:
Unwillingness on the part of our leaders
To invest in human capital because the money
Is earmarked for embezzlement,
And to create moronic personnel their own children

Educated abroad in best schools can keep
The multitude of half-baked personnel
Under their superior control.

968. The Strength And Weakness

Of institutions of countries under democracy flow
From the leaders in government.
Leaders who rule based on rule of law
Will bequeath good governance on their countries
Where things work,
And will serve as template their successors
And heads of institutions will follow and improve upon.
But heads of government who want those heading
The institutions of their countries pander
To their whims by watching body language
And actions before they can perform
Their constitutional duties will render such countries
Weak and unprogressive.

969. Just Suspicion

How billions of naira sleek into the private pockets
Of government officials and those in the corridor of power
Through the ritual of annual budgeting.
Money are allocated for a number of capital projects
But no outsiders know if such money
Are released or not but continue to reappear
In the yearly budgets.
Why for instance pensioners' arrears said to be
In the yearly budgets takes years to implement
In piecemeal?

970. Playing Sycophancy Game

Is a Nigeria's perfected strategy to ensure
Personal wellbeing.

This is why our government officials will not respond
Promptly or not at all to good or bad things
That involve poor members of the public.
But they will rush to rejoice or commiserate,
As the case may be,
With their principals and families.
It is all a demonstration to ensure the safety
Of their daily bread.

971. A Gentleman Leader

Who was not aware of symptom of strange disease
(Or if aware was too naive and weak
To take a position)
Being introduced into the system by his comrades
In government to rip off the commonwealth
Of the people on whose behalf they presided
Over the nation's purse.
The emerging abuse of trust by his lieutenants
Was to be precursor his successors had perfected
To become an endemic cancer in the political
History of the Country.
The charade continued until the jackboot struck
Which removed him permanently from the scene.
He was a gentleman leader who presided
Over the nation's wealth yet died a poor man
With no single house worth a man of his position
His name was Alhaji Tafawa Balewa,
First Prime Minister of independent Nigeria.
The sad commentary is that the same jackboot
That sent legitimately elected government out of office
For graft was the one that set a new height
On which corruption waxed stronger.

972. Fasting

Is a period devoted to moments of spiritual meditations
And sober reflection in human life
To allow the soul commune with the Spirit.
A moment for self reappraisal and denials;
Period of trial for the soul to forsake sins
And vow not to go back to them,
So it can be granted spiritual permission
To gain heaven.

973. Extinction Of Lives

Giving birth to one child is moderating life.
Two can be tolerated but three is a crowd.
Above that is planning overpopulation
And a recipe for extinction of lives
On earth.

974. Bastardized Land

Is what they have turned my country to.
Where equitable service providing is not
A guarantee but arbitrariness a daily occurrence.
The ordinary people have no access
To the minimum good things in the land
But a large dose of the suffering.

975. In Economic Fry-pan

Whose victims are the vulnerable government contractors
And retirees who have no means to defend
Their interest.
Money due for work done by contractors
And pensioners' current and arrears are first lodged
In the private accounts of government officials
For upward of three to six or twelve months
To yield them interest while their unfortunate victims
Remain being fried in economic fry-pan.

976. A Guilty Conscience

Is a spiritual wound in the mind and is deeper
And difficult to heal than flesh wound.
Unless you properly atone for it,
The wound remains unhealed till death.
I run from inflicting a wound of guilt
On my conscience.
While I can endure the human blame
For my actions I cannot endure the blame
Or run away from my guilty conscience.

977. Overpopulation

Without commensurate growth in provisions
To curb poverty
Is a suicidal way to run a country.
Those in charge of governance know this
So they can plan ahead.
But they are victims of greed and ego boosting
That blind them to do what is right

978. I Am The Only Mentally Conscious

When walking or driving in a busy and congested
Traffic.
Do not misunderstand my drift,
But I am the only one who can vouch
For my mental state and be extra careful
Of my surroundings and not pre-empt what other
Person will do next by taking necessary precaution
Against the unexpected.

979. Despair Not,

Consolatory words for those whose fathers are not known
Or refused to claim them.

They must take solace in answering the names
Of their mothers' fathers and mind not
What people may say behind their back
Or to their face.
God who is responsible for our biological creation
Is the only true Father of us all.

980. "Tarred With The Same Brush"

All over in both developed and underdeveloped societies
Politicians lie and steal.
The difference between the two is that politicians
In the developed societies get things done
For the people to avoid searchlight being beamed
On their activities unlike the politicians
In underdeveloped societies.
They do not have moral conscience to judge them.

981. Treated As Tea Party Affairs

Is what governance in Nigeria has always been
By both the military adventurers and
Political opportunists.
The reason why the top seat of government
Is often occupied by unserious politicians
Or who were not prepared for governance.

982. Labyrinth Corridors Of Law

Laws are made supposedly to correct antisocial behaviours
Of the people through judicial adjudication for easy
And sm0oth running of government activities
So we can have decent society to live in.
For reasons that may make sense to legal luminary
Some of the provisions weaved around technical jargon
As if deliberately designed so the legal operators
Can easily be caught in their webs

To the detriment of those seeking justice
Getting the rough edges of law;
But relief to those who inflict injustice.
To the layman they seem to make nonsense
Of equitable dispensation of fairness by creating
Fertile ground for crime to flourish.
In the end dispensation of justice or injustice
Depends on the whims and caprices of law
And not what is right or what is wrong.

983. Two Steps Forward

Three backward will not make the wayfarer
Arrive at a predetermined destination.
This is how best I can characterize my country
As a familiar road the cowboys in uniforms
And the political fortune seekers have
All along been taking her in a merry-go-round
For their sole benefit.

984. Pests And Their Lives.

We kill flies and ants at will;
We kill rats and cockroaches,
And other pests that invade our homes
Without giving a second thought to their lives
Yet they have lives as we do.
Our consolation lies in the fact that
They pester our lives which neutralizes
Our seemly offhand action and absolve us of blames.
If not why do we not kill lizards,
Frogs and others that do not come into
Our homes to endanger our lives?

985. Road To Our Hospitals

Is very difficult to walk and leads to death

For those who have no money to buy
Members of the staff and treatments;
Or know somebody who can facilitate their treatments.
If non of these you might chose to endure
The suffering and perhaps get nothing much
For your troubles.
Or decide to walk the road to death directly
"Without much ado".

986. Who Can Solve The Puzzle

Surrounding high and low profile cases
That involve the high and mighty in the society,
And the ordinary man on the street respectively?
Towards end of March and first day April, 2018
I heard the news that the conference of Judges
Came up with a position that there had not
Been convictions of high profile cases because
Of poor handling and shoddy investigations by the
Prosecuting teams which lack watertight evidence
Before presenting them in courts (Not their exact wording).
But where the ordinary man is accused of
Petty stealing there are always convictions.
Yet the same members of the bench,
The Bar and law officers are involved on
Both sides of the divide.
The shell covering the nut of the high and mighty
In which they hide themselves is too hard to crack,
While the shell covering the nut of ordinary man
Is fragile and easy to break like eggshell.
Who can solve the puzzle?
Of course very easy:
Money and influence make it difficult
And uphill task to crack the hard shell,
Whereas lack of both make it easy to crack

The fragile shell of the later.
Of the three arms one or all are culpable
Of compromise along the line.

987. Free Flow Of The Nation's Currencies

Onto the lap of our political office holders
Is so made possible through the lopsided
And defective way we run our public institutions.
Earnings from industrial activities that oil the wheels
Of the nation's economy are remitted into government coffer,
Otherwise the common purse!
The common purse is supposedly belonged to the people
For their wellbeing and progress of the nation,
In accordance with the provisions of the constitution
And act of parliament.
But since politicians control parliament and the power
To appropriate they have unhindered access
To the vast resources of the nation.
Were it not constraint on them to allocate
Some fractions to public services like capital projects
And salaries for the workforce nothing hardly
Will get back to the people.
Structurally the bulk of the nation's wealth
Flow into the private pockets through leakages,
Like the infamous ten percent kick back!

988. Incapacitated Government

In well organized societies government is stronger
Than individuals.
But in poorly and fraudulently run societies
Individuals are stronger than their government,
And the oppressed people form the bastion
Of strength behind them.
The people's support is rooted in the blind

Hero- worshipping and ethno- centric sentiments.
Ignorantly not knowing their rights or
Too complacent to defend them.
And attituditional helplessness based on what can
We do syndrome.

989. The Whites In God's Own Country

And their litany of hate against their compatriots:
The blacks for their skin colour and their seemingly
Criminal tendencies as they want to believe.
The Jews for their astuteness in commerce
And diplomacy.
The indigenous American Indians they relegate
To second class citizens in their own God
Given land.

990. Serving Wine In Golden Goblet

Is symbolic allowing Spirit of God rule your heart
And you will walk the right path to glory.
If you put faith in your own wisdom alone
Is like a man trying to fetch water
With a basket.

991. Errand Boys

Is the level to which heads of government
In underdeveloped countries have reduced themselves
As if they are vassal to these foreign leaders.
Every now and then we hear the news
That these heads of government jetting out
At the invitation from the leaders of the advanced countries.
Yet we do not hear these underdeveloped countries' leaders
Inviting the leaders of advanced countries,
Even to come and see their underdevelopment.

992. Suicide

Is a self murder and an abominable act;
A curse on whosoever terminates his own life
He has no power to create thereby commits
Heinous crime against nature.
The person is a downright coward bereft of ideas
How to manage and control the intrigues of life
To his best advantages.
He lacks courage to face rigorous challenges of life;
Fearful soldier upon merely hearing rumour of war
Deserts the war zone.

993. The Philosophy Of Paradise On Earth

Is developed and practiced by the consortium
Of embezzlers and fraudsters,
Murderers for cash and all the related crimes
For acquisitions of wealth.
These greedy people cannot afford to suffer want
On earth and wait for paradise in heaven
Which they do not even believe exists.
And if they do cannot be bothered to worry
About it here on earth.
So they create their own paradise here

994. Eating Big For Its Worth

I have heard millions and billions being embezzled
And stolen by privileged people in high places.
Whether they will suffer punishment in heaven or not
Is to nobody's knowledge.
But the looters are certainly enjoying paradise
On earth.
I will be stupid to steal measly thousands
Which will not afford me good life here on earth
And still feel the guilt of punishment in heaven,

Which may perhaps be or not be.
However,
Everybody has an appointment to Keep with retributive justice.

995. Overconfidence

Is a self-defeatist mistake a hero can make
To fall a victim to less stronger opponent:
It makes him unwary and tactless in his move.
Overrating your strategy and strength but underrate
That of your opponent is bound to cause your fall.
By the time you realize it you may have
Met your downfall.
This happens not only in physical combat
But also in mental exercise.

996. All Are Interdependent

Since all biological components in the body
Are interdependent for harmonious functioning
of life in an organism.
So also are the various segments of a corporation
And other organizations,
From the cleaner to the top management hierarchy,
Are interdependent for maximal and effective functioning
Otherwise the corporation will be in a total mess.
Therefore all sectors should be recognized and well respected
As being equally important and relevant for the progress
Of the corporation

997. A Pot Of Porridge

Can be used to describe the ever available
Potentials of our land.
Though it boasts of huge sources of revenue
Our leaders lack foresight and forward planning
leaders lack foresight and forward planning

To harness its many abundant yields for the benefit
Of all.
They only concentrate on a single source
Of revenue which had hitherto drawn the jackboot
Adventurers to its pot of porridge like the moths
To a pool of light.
They had their field day of exploitation of its pudding.
And now in civilian garb in collaboration
With the politicians are still dipping their hands
Into our pot of porridge.

998. Politicking With People's Lives

Is a stock-in-trade game for our politicians,
The reason why policy issues meant to benefit
The people are treated with levity and disdain.
They play politics for their own gain and self relevance,
Not to benefit the people which is supposed
To be the main reason why in politics
And in government.
Theirs is a false democracy to blindfold the people
So they can manipulate them through religion
And ethnic sentiments.
Our people's lukewarm attitude to matters concerning
Their lives give those in government the leeway
To sideline them from their legitimate rights.
It is all about settlement for favoured members
Of the political party in power.

999. Three Deadly Intoxicant Investitures

Dangerous to possess by an individual are position,
Power and freedom.
These three should not be invested on one
Individual person who can easily misuse any
If he is of unbalanced mind.

He is easily swayed by such possessions and
Tend to believe all his decisions are based
On a sound judgment.

1000. Weak Government

Is usually unable to enforce its national policies.
The people become lawless and the ones who
Bear the brunt.
One example is inability to enforce the use
Of our naira and kobo coin denominations,
Thereby increasing inflation level.

1001. Chief Executives In Government

(And their deputies)
Mr. President - Head of government of a country,
And symbol of unity as father-head.
Their Excellencies - Governors the chief executives
Of their respective States.
Senators - Members of the country's senate.
Honourables -- Members of the House of Representatives,
States Houses of Assembly who are often
In the pockets of the governors;
Chairmen and councilors whose presence
Are not felt by the people
Except to collect dues on shops and other charges.
By virtue of the unique position as the country's
Chief executive Mr. President must be humble
And rational in his actions.

1002. Irredeemable Failure.

You are accused of not making progress
As your better neighbours but you are comparing
Yourself with the never do well.
If you persist in this lackluster attitude to life

You are definitely heading for irredeemable failure.

1003. Economic Blindfold

Being practiced by our political gladiators:
They will declare with relish that the economy
Has improved due to physical measures government adopts.
They then tell us with glee that inflation rate
Has gone down.
But the reality of the whole scenario
Is played out by the market forces.
Get certain items today and go back the second day
Or the third day for the same items
The prices have increased marginally.
Who is fooling whom?
We Should now be wise.
Unfortunately some of us hapless citizens
Still lend themselves to be led by the nose.

1004. Sticklers To Traditions

To preserve their past heritage and the memories
Of their forefathers and the great empire
For the generations coming after them.
Were all the countries in the world to do away
With their cultures and customs and adopt
The modern trend of life these proud sticklers
To traditions will not – come rain or shine.
They are proud of their past heritage
Yet still manage to blend together both ancient
And modern life to suit their psyche.
If you are that type of a discerning mind
You know them.

1005. Groping For Reality

Though we know what and how to grasp it
Our selfishness has so far denied us
The opportunity.
We are a people ever lastly in search
Of national cohesion to make us one united people
but tribalism,
religion and host of other practices
have so far kept us separate we are unable
to attain nationhood

1006. Big Men Nemesis

Is stress which subjects them to severe shock
Due to unexpected change of fortune.
No matter how well and hearty they appear to be
They easily succumb.
They live in the false world of their own
And make themselves gods above the laws
Of the land.
They feel so secure and immune from punishments,
At least here on earth.
So when unfortunate to be arraigned for criminal charges
They easily collapse under stress
Because their exalted position and soft living
Have stripped them of resistance to acute pressure.

1007. Heaven On Earth

Shall come when people in any assemblage,
Be it religious gathering,
Business forum and other informal meetings
Where after end of deliberations people will depart
Without some taking away what do not belong
To them.
For example some items forgotten behind by guests.
We shall be hoping that some day

Heaven shall begin to reign on earth.

1008. Let Us Be Good

To ourselves for it will make us good,
And the world a merry-go-round for us all.
We shall no more have the cause
To wish for heaven for then it is already
With us on earth.

1009. Discredited Politicians

Are in every country but mostly prevalent
In developing economy.
If there are few who have no inclinations
To be discredited and corrupt the system
Will compromise them.
You cannot be in government and be apolitical!

1010. When To Be Anti-Christ Or Mohammed

In relating to the true practice of religion
For the benefit of mankind.
Not many will openly admit practicing traditional religion,
Unless Christianity or Mohammedanism.
But whenever it suits the Christians and Moslems
They put aside religion and opt
For maximum profits at the expense
Of their customers.
It is then they become anti-Christ and Mohammed
In practice.

1011. Every Language Is Clumsy

And difficult unless you are able to understand
And speak it.
Therefore it is pointless to criticize any language
Or dialect as gibberish simply because

You do not understand it.

1012. Guiltless Conscience

Will harvest peace of mind for restful living.
Iwill therefore always spare my enemy if he
Or she happens to fall my victim.
Not for his or her sake but for mine.
I wish for a clean mind so I can live
A free life with a guiltless conscience.

1013. Unlike An Active Volcano

Which from its molten core erupts
A hot lava cascading down from the peak
In a river of liquid fire showing nature
In its violent displeasure.
The average of my compatriot has dormant volcano
In him which no amount of provocations
From his inept government will ever stir
To erupt,
Not even mildly,
Content as always a decoy beast.

1014. Law Of Cause And Effect

Is a Universal Order under which matter is controlled.
When there is a cause there follows an effect
It Is erroneously assumed that when a man
Does good he has the blessings of God
or evil the backing of devil.
Nothing like that in nature.
Our good and evil deeds are attuned to
The Law of Cause and effect
The results from either
You reap what you Sow

1015. A Recalcitrant Child

In the house has his day of usefulness"
Says our common proverb.
He will not want the family fall victim
Of other miscreants.
A thief in the community is the chief security
Officer in his area and will not allow other thieves
Operate in his domain.
He knows he will be a first suspect
Unless he is of a deprave character.

1016. Haaaaaaa!

My mouth cannot close again from shock
For the monumental plundering of my country's
Vast wealth my ears have heard and eyes
Have witnessed.
The humongous wastes of her resources
And the harrowing experience of the naked pillage
By her few favoured individuals.

1017. A Religious Mind

Was man created from beginning?
How else did the primitive ancestors
In my remote village who never heard,
Much less exposed to Western religion,
Know about God?
So man was albinitio created a religious mind,
And he created the personality of God!

1018. Cost Of Doing Business Here

Is very high and cutthroat competitive venture.
Starting with high cost of petroleum products
And sometimes non availability of them,
Bad roads to transport goods and people conveniently

To and fro.
Non availability of good rail system for the haulage
Of hardware products from ports to other locations.
All manner of government officials
Manning countless checkpoints forcefully demanding
Bribes from transporters.
The cost of all these are passed down
To the end-users.
All these add to make my country
One of the most where cost of living
Is very high and excruciating experience
That proves true the saying:
Survival of the fittest!"

1019. The Black Diamonds

And their flair for music and sporting uniqueness. flair)
The Yoruba proverb says:
"Out of the black pot comes the white pap".
So it is with our black brothers and sisters
In God's own country and elsewhere.
History taught us that every human race
Has its own unique gift of talent
Irrespective of colour and creed.
Was it the bitter experience of slavery
That inspired the flair for music and sport?
We can do no less than salute them,
Not for dominating the two fields
Of human endeavours
But for giving the world and humankind
The pleasure of their best efforts.

1020. Three Cardinal Points

To observe in fighting crime are prevention,
Apprehension and application of appropriate

And corrective punishment.
No society is crime free and can eradicate it
Because where human beings co-exist
There must be deviant elements.
Law must be abreast and beat the rate down,
Ever as it is impossible to eliminate it.

1021. Intellectual Stigmatization

Against poor achiever because he is prejudged incapable
Of intelligent idea of producing intellectual work.
His work is hidden in contempt and denied exposure.
Nobody cares to reason that he may have done
A good intellectual work worth the attention
Of the world.

1022. A Very Trusting Person

Is a gullible somebody who has no reservoir
Of checks and balances.
He is easily dazzled and sway with the trappings
Of personal appearance without weighing the hidden
Characters of the person.

1023. Imitation Life.

In saner societies leaders provide affordable shelters
For the people,
Abundant flow of water for commercial and
Social conveniences that make life comfortable.
But in less transparent climes all the amenities
Are luxuries beyond the reach of ordinary citizens
Except few who can source them.
Here we lead life of imitation.

1024. Between Responsibility And Deceit.

Every political party that comes to power in this country

Works in the same pattern like its predecessors.
Self interest is the foremost driving force to enrich
Those who is who in the inner circle,
Those in the periphery of power and
The general interest of the party.
Their style of governance is running helter shelter
Pretending to be doing a lot without doing nothing.
As the same human species all over this scenario
Can be played out in other climes.
But the people over there know their right
And fight for it.
The leaders on their own provide Some basic things.

1025. If Swearing To God

Is a sure guarantee to prove innocence
There is no single criminal in the world.
Caught with or without the goods on them they
Find it convenient to swear in the name of God
To plead their innocence to escape justice.
Because God is not available to prove or disprove
This time honoured ignoble route to plead innocence

1026. Shock Absorber

Against the unexpected should it happen
Against all your hopes.
Do not put all faith and hope on something valuable
That is yet not in your hands.
Steer the middle course that all expectations
May or may not be realized,
So that when the unexpected disappointment happens
You will not be too disappointed.

1027. Vicious Circle

In which our stakeholders steer the affairs of

Our country by selling off at giveaway prices
Our common assets to friends and cronies
In the name of privatization and commercialization.
The vicious circle is that these public enterprises
Belonging to the people are being funded by those
In power with our common wealth without
Commensurate good services.
The profits revolve around in their circle and
The people are left with little or nothing.

1028. Planning To Be An Achiever

Through educational failure because you have seen
Or heard others achieved greatness by it is
A self delusion.
Failing educationally in early life as a dropout
To become an achiever in later years
Is not by design but accidental.
If you plan to follow the same line
So you may become a great achiever
You are planning your life disaster.
No sane person will do that!

1029. Material Or Spiritual Empire,

Which category do you really belong?
Many people love building material empire around themselves
While only few are building spiritual and intellectual empire.
One vital truth is that spiritual and intellectual empire
Will outlive material things.
Spiritual and intellectual works will reverberate
Through generations:
Their noble contributions give value to life.

1030. Paper Qualification Not Efficiency.

Many otherwise good jobs have been bungled

Because leaders on the seat of power
Prefer paper qualification to efficiency.
Efficiency is thus sacrificed for paper qualification
By placing inept but educated charlatans in key position.
Of course,
Those in positions of authority do not want efficiency
But a safe haven to run their “chop and I chop"
Administration.

1031. Headquarter Of Crimes

Always rumbles with staccato bursts of gunfire
And screech of tyres on the asphalt roads,
Chasing horde of criminals through the metropolis.
Crimes are being committed on daily basis
In every corner of the globe
But the crime rate in the land of the "policeman"
Of the world leads the pack!

1032. A Country Gone To The Dogs,

Who picks the fat from the carcass?
Politicians and religious leaders!
The politicians go before the pastors to seek
For spiritual blessings to cover their exploitative tracks,
And pastors enjoy huge proceed from tithes
And other donations by the congregation everlastingly
Seeking for a twig of hope to make
The elusive breakthrough to prosperity.
Hardwork and sincerity by both leaders
And the led save a country to achieve
National and personal breakthrough.

1033. Absurd Thought.

Man can most times pitifully be absurd and
Foolish in his way of thinking and carry out

His thoughts in actions.
How can a man in his right mind kill human
Lives created by God and claimed justified
Killing the same lives for His sake or for Him.
It sounds insane idea!

1034. Contingency Plan

Is a very important option in running one's business.
A man who plans a line of action without
Contingency plan should the original fail to materialize
May likely fall into a deep gorge.
Any man with foresight must always have an
Alternative plan of action to fall back on.
Like the night prowler rodent wise enough
To dig an emergency escape exit.

1035. Analogue Or Digital,

Which one do you go for as a youth
Of this present jet age?
You cannot afford to lag behind in this
Fast moving shift to the age of digital technology
For the future world.
The world is moving fast to catch up and
As the youth of the future you should
Find yourself there and leave analogue
To old timers.

1036. Response To Madman's Abuse

Is a confirmation to your own state of mind.
A confirmed madman calls you a madman
And you respond in any form means the madman
Is correct.
Your response confirms your brain disorder.

1037. Death To The Rescue.

You have a great idea you nurse to actualize
But for one reason or the other you are unable
To carry it out before your death.
You no longer have to worry because
You are no more in a position to,
For death has relieved you of worry.

1038. Lost Our Originality

And opt for the traditions of the foreign lands.
We today copy wrongly virtually every culture
We watch on TV,
Thereby robbing us of our original roots.
While these foreign lands showcase their rich cultures,
We may in future have nothing to show
If we persist in this ignoble pursuit.

1039. A Victim Of Dual Nationality

You belong to because your father married a native
Of a big town or another country he happens
To be residing.
The people of your mother hold your father's birth place
With lowly views and with derogatory epithet.
You join in because you are so proud
Of your mother's noble birthplace you belong.
You are equally affected having in your veins
The blood of your father.
You cannot wash away the abusive smear
With mere wish as also a victim.

1040. What Tomorrow For Old Man?

Cautioning an old man of seventy and above
To eat sparingly because there is tomorrow
Is ill-advised and wicked.

What tomorrow does an old man of such age
Have but to live for today and be expecting
His last day?

1041. **Lest Morality Takes Complete Flight**
From our land
Hence I repeat stringently my clarion call.
We are systematically sacrificing our cultural heritage
On the altar of Western religion and civilization.
We appeal to traditionalists and cultural groups
In our dear land to salvage our cultures and customs
From the vice grip of foreign influence we have embraced.
They should please keep the torch of our cultures
And customs brightly alight so we do not sink
Into moral decadence.
Should that day come we shall not be only
A lost people but also at a point of death
Without identity as a people.

1042. **Your Responsibilities Not Mine,**
The way every new incoming government in Nigeria
Runs its policies.
The new incoming government,
Whether the same party but headed by new man
Or whether another party,
Is sure to abandon the agenda of the outgoing
Government and sets its own new agenda.
All in effort to boost self-importance
As the new man in charge.
Perhaps this does not happen here alone
But Nigeria will top the list of countries
With number of abandoned or uncompleted projects.

1043. **International Maestro**

Whose melodious voice reverberated through every nook
And cranny of our land and international arena.
His music was so unique that it attracted the attention
Of the Queen of England to earn him
The prestigious honour as a member of British Empire.
His name: Isaac Kehinde Dairo!

1044. Positive Force Vs Negative Force

Are incompatible as light and darkness any day.
Your positive spirit,
If you can spiritually employ it,
Will overcome the negative spirit of your enemy.

1045. No Man Should Trust Himself

Until the litmus test of temptation has been overcome.
Man can fall even when he does not want to be
Unconsciously under any unexpected and acute pressure
And overpowering temptation no matter how strong minded
He thinks himself to be.
It would have happened before his senses come
Back to focus reality.
That is when regret comes in.

1046. Burying The Dead

Is a mere gesture of removing the dirt from sight.
Whether you celebrate it with funfair or lowly
The significant aspect is the residual respect
Or shame remains with the mourners.
Easing your faeces into pit latrine or the toilet
All go into the pit to turn to soil.

1047. An Idle Nation

Which uses every excuse to declare workfree days,
Thereby shutting down the economy,

Will earn itself an acute poverty and remain
In an economic limbo.
The private entrepreneurs who must produce daily
Pay overtime to their workforce.
The overhead costs are pass to the end users
Who bear the brunt.
So also a person who regards every unwarranted opportunities
As time for relaxation will rot away
In perpetual want.

1048. Born A Leader.

Politicians are not real leaders but who manipulate
The people's fear and ignorance to hold them captive.
Real leaders in politics are not professional politicians
But born to be leaders.

1049. Ambition

Is the superlative motivator of success.
A non ambitious person is worse than a lazy man.
It is ambition that will push you to the pinnacle
Of your career.
The weapons that aid ambition to realize its objectivities
Are hardwork and perseverance,
Infallible calculation and accurate decisions,
And cool headedness to avoid failure.

1050. The Principle Of Majority

Having their way and the minority their say
Has been redesigned by the ruling class
In this land.
Here the majority have their say
And the few minority in power their way.

1051. Music Of The Winds

And the dance of the leaves.
As I sit by my window
I watch the dance of the leaves
To the silent music of the winds
Telling us in their silent language the beauty
Of the world.

1052. Letter "T"

Is the key to unravel the puzzle.
If the human species were to be without
This fundamental member of the body,
Those who render valuable services to humanity
Would not have been able to do so,
And we would have had nothing in the world
To enjoy.
In like manner those who commit crimes
Could not have been doing so,
And the world would have been rid of crimes.

1053. Logic On Its Head.

In all parts of the world the first born
Of a set of twins is the senior.
But in one part of Nigeria the people
Regard the first to be born the messenger
Of the last who thereby becomes the senior.
This is logic standing on its head!
The identity of the race begins with alphabetical
Letter "Y".
May be a joke at the expense of the last born.

1054. **Man The Warmonger**

Craves fighting wars and to win victories.
But in his true nature
He does not want total victory and absolute conquest.

Because,

If he succeeds making the rest humankind his vassal,

Who is he going to fight with?

This is his dilemma.

1055. Revolt Of The Low Denizens.

If the animals we slaughter for consumption,

Both of the wild and domestic,

Have foreknowledge and reminiscence of events

Of the past

Would have revolted in protest against the atrocities

Committed by men on their lives

By the turn of the centuries.

Of course,

It is their destiny for their venison to grace

The dining table of man.

1056. The Abami Eda

Yoruba words which mean "weird creature "

Was born into an enlightened and radical family

Clan of doctors.

But his radicalism led him into the world of music

To create his own unique brand: The Afro Beat.

He was a prophet of our time,

Fearless in criticism of those holding the reign of power

In a corrupt system created by them,

And also the lethargic apathy of the people

Who allowed themselves be led by the nose.

He was a poison to the corrupt clique

In a corrupt system.

His name was Fela Anikulapo (Ransom) Kuti.

Adieu!

The Afro Beat king,

The black President they love to hate,

Hate to love!

1057. Saddam Hussein,

Nebuchadnezzar incarnate or a false claim?
Although through him history did repeat itself:
He reined with absolute power
And fell from grace to grass!
But unlike Nebuchadnezzar he did not rise from the grass.
"He was dragged,
Bearded and disheveled from a hole in the ground"
Without offering a semblance of resistance
Befitting a hero he was reputed to be.
A hero who became a coward and fainthearted
To allow himself be captured,
Unlike Osama Bin Laden,
Like a rat that has fallen into a dirty water
Without a fight to defend his heroism
Is not qualified as a hero.

1058. Comparative Analysis Of Wickedness

Between the denizens of the wild
And the cognitive man of the civilized society.
The wickedness of the animal is instinctively brutal
But that of man is based on purposeful calculations
And subtly lethal.

1059. All Are Intelligent

In their individual natural way.
A growing plant will dodge around an obstacle
On its way up as a sensible human being
Or animal will do against obstacle on his
Or its path.

1060. Eternal Oblivion

Of the soul after death would have been
The best rest.
But the best arrangement remains in the hands
Of the sole Arbiter of life and death!

1061. With The Award Of Laurels

In our minds we salute men and women
Who sacrificed their comfort and convenience,
Some their lives,
To invent or found new things which have
Continued to benefit humanity.
Without their contributions the world would still
Have remained a modern jungle.

1062. The Yankees In Uncle Sam Country

Are boastful in words and actions internationally
And live by their boast,
They dictate the pace of international politics
Which makes Uncle Sam the "policeman" of the world.

1063. Board Members

Is just a call for the boys and girls
In and periphery of the party in power
To come and "chop".
If and when corporations,
Departments and agencies are embroiled
In operational crises
The presence of the boards into which they are appointed
Are not felt.
Or perhaps passed resolutions government ignored.
It makes the wheels of running the organizations
Turn in circles instead of running progressively forward.

1064. Undue Opportunity To Pilfer.

That product in your pocket you took out
Without official permission because you are not searched
By the security personnel at the gate
Because of your official status
Nevertheless makes you a thief.

1065. "Rumbles In The Jungle".

That was the fight of the century that was.
The apes and the monkeys,
The baboons and the rest of them
Were falling apart by the wayside,
And the lion (king) came out victorious - Muhammad Ali.

1066. Heads Of Key Institutions,

Past and present,
Nurse wounded conscience for the role they played
In the line of their duties.
They are used to carry out state's secret assignments
Not in the books.
As compensation they live big.

1067. Identical Fingerprint.

A man searching for a woman of the same
Blood group to marry will find as many
As he wants.
Not so for a man who insists on marrying
A woman of the same identical fingerprint with him
Will never marry.
Not even were it possible to get the fingerprints
Of those who had come and gone
Since the time of the first man.
A mystery of creation!

1068. A Paradise Treatment.

Give a man all the goodies he needs
In which he will do no work,
Engage in sport and other activities
But just to eat,
Sex and such other pleasure at his disposal
He will after awhile revolt.
The nature of man,
Even the animal thoroughly rejects non activities

1069. Point Of Insanity!

Found the most stupid and dangerous ideology today
Many people will embrace it and become disciples.
It proves that the world has always been
At the point of insanity!

1070. Impulsive Reflex

Dictates that when a hot coal drops on you
And your child or loved one,
Your immediate reaction is to flick it away
From your own body first
Before your child or loved one.
It is a natural reaction instinctively obeyed
By everybody.

1071. Make Themselves Holier

Before God by both Christians and Moslems.
Those who regard themselves who is who
in the society occupy the front pew and arrange
Themselves in the front line behind the Chief Imam.
Yet the minds of most may be darker than those
Who occupy the back seat.

1072. Stumbling Block

Is created by a lot of people
For themselves through laziness,
Sentiment and I don't care attitude,
Of treating every important issues.
The result will surely be to stumble against
The block created by themselves.

1073. No Fool

Will put a rope around his own neck
To be hanged when his country's weak
And corrupt institutions are serving his interest.
No reason why those who run such country
Will want to strengthen their institutions
In a hurry.

1074. Died Once Twice Certified.

This is the subterfuge route most Nigerians
Who leave services of private companies pass through
To steal their own legal entitlements bad policies
Of government have denied them by faking
Their own death.
Otherwise forced to wait till the purported right age
When they are no longer useful,
And paid in piecemeal money equally useless.

1075. Backdoor Drain Pipes.

Our refineries have backdoor drain pipes
Through which the turn-around maintenance
Morey are funneled into.
Your guess is as good as mine.
If it is a lie tell me why they have all
These years refused to turn profitably around.

1076. The Euphoria Of Office

will make an unprincipled man behave like
A former servant to a king on whose head
Providence puts a crown and swore to rule
As a despot.
What do you expect?
Somebody not used to drinking alcohol will easily
Be intoxicated and misbehave.

1077. The Knife And The Yam.

It is morally bound on you who hold
The proverbial knife and the yam allow yourself
Be cheated rather than using your fortunate position
Cheat your vulnerable victims.
Those with greedy nature will not permit
Their conscience tow this moral line.

1078. Iron Armour

Is what the man aiming to beard the lion
In its den will need.
A profitable advice for over ambitious mind
Who aims to conquer the world of materialism.

1079. Discretion Begets Wisdom

When faced with a dilemma of action.
Which do you choose in a nasty situation
If your reasoning goes for discretion
But your bravado chooses valour?
Discretion will give valour the wisdom
To overcome a dicey situation.

1980. EFCC'S Note Of Lessons,

Building an enviable history for future generation.
High profile cases involving the big shots

In our society have become celebrated farce
Of dramatic episodes for future study.

1081. Political Stooges Hobnob,
Dine and wine with the politicians
And powers that be.
Their words and actions influence government
Policies negatively because their agenda
Is to feather their own nest.

1082. Connections.
Though ethical equity frowns at it,
In both developed and underdeveloped societies,
Most people get what they want through connections.
A fact of life we are forced to live with.

1083. The Menace Of Overpopulation
of the human species on earth will be
A major epidemic we may not be able to control.
We can control rate of birth if we desire it
But we cannot control rate of death.
Yet overpopulation is threatening to overwhelm
The entire world.

1084. Elections Fallout
In my country is an episode of the absurd.
An average politician seeking election into an
Elective post is a winner before election day.
After elections and results are declared
The losers accuse winners of rigging.
For all their accusations and counter accusations
There are no genuine winners or losers
On either side.

1085. Government Nonchalant Attitude

Towards rendering qualitative and transparent services
To the people through its corrupt officials
Makes corruption a viable enterprise.

1086. Panel-beaten Out Of Shape.

The majority of our people have their lives
Panel beaten out of shape by government bad policies.
And if good they are subjected to arbitrary
Implementations by its corrupt officials.

1087. When Temporarily Alive

For those who cannot afford to eat their choice
Of food but await,
With keen expectations,
The approach of festive periods.
Their days of temporarily been alive.

1088. Be Warned

And always beware to avoid situations that will
Make you gasp and try to clutch at the twigs
To save yourself.
Therefore "forewarned is forearmed".

1089. In A Dilemma

Of making a choice between two beautiful women
You equally love, your best decision
Must be based on character.
But beware of false character intended
To deceive you.

1090. Man Dreads Change.

Yet he is quick to demand for it when confined
To a regular routine

Because his behaviours change like the chameleon.
Put him in a place within seconds
He has changed position.

1091. **Broadway Of Knowledge.**

When light arrives darkness disappears for people
To see their way.
When knowledge is gained ignorance disappears
And people will know their right.
When you educate the youths you are educating
The nation for personal and national
Development and progress.

1092. **Survival.**

Nature gives every organic creature sustenance
Of livelihood.
While human beings do physical work to feed
Animal and others forage for the same purpose,
And plants through their roots seep nourishing moisture
From the soil.
All in a beehive activities for survival!

1093. **Survival Instincts**

Sway our loyalty more strongly towards
Those we believe can promote our interest
Than political,
Religious or blood relationship affiliation.

1094. **Rubbished By Civilization**

Which has robbed our minds the sense
Of moral standard,
And planted in us the seed of greed
And deceit.

1095. No End In Sight

To bad rubbish in my dear country.
Those things mostly used by the common people
Are often out of their reach
Because the government in place does not care
About their welfare.

1096. Unless The Taproot

Is uprooted the poisonous tree will continue
To grow and spread its tentacles of branches,
The synonym for terrorist or any fratricidal movement.
Any underground movement has the backing of its financials -
Arresting and killing the foot soldiers is merely
Clipping off few branches of the contagious tree.

1097. A Flaming Sword.

Religion is supposed to be a soothing ointment
To heal our spiritually ailing souls.
But the sons of men continue to employ it
As flaming sword to pierce our hearts.
Religion is the most volatile topic
You do not stir its hornet's nest.
So "let the sleeping dog lie undisturbed".

1098. Made To Suffer Ignominious Death

The ilk used to record the death sentence
of the Ogoni 9 had yet to dry
When they were executed.
Yet some hardened criminals on death row
Who had carried arms against the state and
Found guilty of gruesome murder are still living.
What a pity!

1099. A Million Years Ahead

For man on earth what will his score card
Likely going to be?
How judiciously will he make use of the land
Bequeathed to him?
History will tell if he will reduce it to a
Concrete mass through his greedy acquisition
For commercial and residential structures,
But leaving no arable land to cultivate
For farming to sustain life.
Not a prediction of doom but a foresight
Into the future of man and his world.

1100. Nature's Unpredictabilities.

Nature maintains regular evolutionary pattern
Except when it displays some creative freaks
Known as inconsistencies or errors of nature,
Hence the good and the bad,
The beautiful and the ugly!
Sometimes these oddities occur through interferences
From the evil activities of men and women.

1101. Self-preservation From Danger,

Like the hot coal,
You, instinctively shied away from it
To save yourself before you think of others.
Though on a deeper consideration you can die
To save a beloved one,
But under a sudden danger the immediate reaction
Is first to save yourself before others.

1102. President Without Sceptre

Who was not allowed to rule by the reactionary cabal.
He rolled out his welfare package for the people

And knowing his philanthropic antecedent,
The people for once put aside their religious
And ethnic sentiments and cast their votes for him.
But the reactionaries didn't want it and scuttled
The mandate freely given to him by the people
Thereby robbed the people the chance for good governance.
Not only that, they made sure he was removed permanently.
With time he was vindicated and made a president
Who did not rule.
Chief Moshood Kasimawo Olawale Abiola (aka MK0).

1103. A Political Arena

Is what our leaders have turned the church to.
It has become a pastime and a game for them
To use the pulpit as a podium
For government policy statements.
It does not augur well for the church
Or the nation that regards itself practicing secularism.
They want to be seen as Godly
Yet do not know the colour of God

1104. Divine Intervention

Is an act of God which delivered Daniel
From the jaws of lions;
It delivered Shadrach, Meshach and Abednego
From Nebuchadnezzar's inferno.
Divine intervention will always deliver
Those who righteously deserve it
From precarious situations.

1105. The Three Pillars

On which development and progress of a nation
Must stand are security of life and property,
Vibrant economy and qualitative education.

These three sectors are the bases and the kernel
Of growth of any nation.
It is the duty of a good government
Headed by a quality leadership to bestow
These three institutional legacies on the people
To impact positively on their lives
And move the country forward.

1106. Kissing Culture

Is an 'unAfrican' thing, the copy-cat morons
Who must ape everything foreign are suffering
From inferiority complex.
The African man enjoys to see and playfully
Smack the shaking buttocks or fondle the breasts
of his African damsel with pride.

1107. No Organic Creature

That procreates through engaging in sexual act
Can do so were sex a tedious and unpleasant experience.
Only few would care to engage in it
And the population of every species would have
Been very nominal.
The world would have been spared the scourge
Of overpopulation.

1108. Voluntary Resignation

In the face of weighting allegation
Is not a Nigerian habit.
In other lands merely mentioning government
Top official in connection with abuse of office
Is enough to resign honourably.
Here we do not have the honour
To tow this honourable line unless we are forced.
Any Nigerian top official,

Indeed African who resigned voluntarily without cajole
Maybe seen as a coward or not true son
Or daughter of the soil.

1109. In My Grandfather's Compound

Today the world is in my grandfather's compound
Where every member of the extended families can see
Talk and go into each other's room.
They call it the global village!

1110. Wandering Mind

Is when different thoughts keep assailing your mind
Bordering on endearing frivolities and foreboding issues.
It usually happens when your subconscious mind
Is not constructively focusing on serious issues
Of the day.
This scenario happens at night during waking moments
And find it difficult to go back to sleep.

1111. Risk In Trust

As we can hardly know who to trust
In this present world of materialism.
Yet the world boasts of millions of worship
Houses of different religions and denominations,
All calling on God.

1112. Your Rights

And the mindset of uncouth armed law officials,
How far do they go in underdeveloped environment
Operating outside the rule of law?
They spare bullets for armed bandits and expend them
On innocent citizens.
You cannot be brave in a lawless society
To prove a point.

We have witnessed innocent individuals being cut down
By armed law officials with or without provocations.
To be brave armed officials in lawless environment
Is needlessly offering yourself as a martyr.

1113. Existence!

If and when eventually God decides to end life,
Including the universe,
What will be in place?
Nothingness?
And where will nothingness exist?
The questions and answers man cannot even begin
To imagine and they agonize the mind.
If there is a beginning God is that beginning,
And if no more existence
God remains the Beginning!

1114. Election Blue.

Both the local and international monitoring
And observer groups see what are on the table
In the conduct of elections,
Especially in underdeveloped countries
Where elections must be won at all cost.
The deal under the table they cannot see
As you cannot see the underneath ripples
In a muddy river.

1115. Just The State Of Mind

To feel awesome fear of the dead body
Of human being.
The dead body is just like someone asleep,
Therefore nothing fearful about it.

1116. The Big Rivers

Are overflowing their banks like a deluge
Caused by heavy rainfall.
The excess water is from the tributaries of hundreds
Of small rivers feeding the big ones,
Which as a result are getting dried.
The analogy applies to my country's legislative members,
The political appointees and a motley of aides
Who have undeserved privilege to earn the highest
Pay and allowances in a poorly managed economy,
Leaving the poor working class and the country
In an abject poverty by the day.

1117. Corruption Witch

Is truly hunting and sucking the blood
Of the opposition members,
And its snout is dripping blood.
The witch master has urged those in opposition camps
To come under the witch coven to escape
The bite of the prowling witch.
A tantalizing carrot!

1118. No Devil Without Man

A man marooned on a desert or in the jungle
Will have no devil to fear.
Once he admits the sons of men
He has admitted devil.
A man who is alone cannot be a devil;
He needs another man to play the devil.

1119. Evil Agents.

Life is full of mysteries and some of them
Are caused by the evil spirits.
These evil spirits as well as good spirits
Do not act by themselves

But through bad people who harness
And employ the evil power to do their bidding
And good people use spiritual power
To counteract the work of evil people.

1120. Spilled Milk

If you have taken an unpleasant action
That has gone haywire against expectations
There is no need moaning over it.
As they say:
"No need crying over spilled milk".
And "Let bygone be bygone
If no solution to counter the deed
The best solution is forget about it.
If that fails do not talk about it.

1121. Language Extinction

Is imminent in Nigeria by the turn of this century,
And it is going to affect both major languages
And dialects at the rate every family adopts
English as the lingua franca of the fatherland
Unless we beat a retreat.
It is one thing to use English as a medium
Of communication between federating units
But quite another matter to adopt it
As a mother tongue.

1122. I Will Fly

But we have not seen you develop wings
Much less literally flying to the promised land
And take the people along with you.
The familiar promise by our rulers:
I will do this I will do that,
Already the people are trek wearing.

1123. Common Property

Owned by everybody is the ground.
Nobody born anywhere or under whatever circumstances
That will not land on the ground.
Whether it is your ancestral land,
Bought or rented you are owner of a portion
Of the ground where you will live and be buried.
Nobody is born to live in the air
Or on the water.

1124. "Before Abraham Was.....

I AM".
Yet the so-called men of God,
Like the Jews of old,
Do not understand that it was God
The Creator that spoke
Literally saying:"I created Abraham!"

1125. He Failed The Test of History

When the agents of change came knocking at the door.
Instead of listening to their message and negotiate
For peaceful reforms he hauled invective abuses at them
And called their bluff.
He failed to learn from their neighbour Algeria
Where agents of change first struck.
He was intoxicated by the trappings of power
So Muammar Gaddafi went down for ignoring history,
Despite he had done well for the people.

1126. GOWON:

'Go on with one Nigeria
Is a task that must be done'.
That was the slogan of the civil war between

Nigeria and Biafra led by Gen. Yakubu Gowon
And Colonel Odumegwu Ojukwu (1967-70).
The sorrow tale till date is that the military-cum-civilian
Politicians in charge of the united Nigeria
Are toying with her destiny,
They have so far failed to keep the hard-won
Unity with the innocent blood of our men and women
Firmly united and prosperous.

1127. Religious And Political Animal.

Every human being is first religious
And political anima! before anything else.
All his actions are directed by these
Two ideological philosophies.
Abinitio religion and politics are offshoot
Of traditions and customs which are
The basic roots of his life,
Be it civilized or primitive setting.

1128. Who Gains From War?

Definitely not the winning side or losing side.
Both sides suffer loss of lives and properties,
Bodily and emotional damages.
And the most vulnerable to losses are the women
And the children on both sides.
The ultimate gainer of war is the supplier
Of weapons of war,
The behind the screen schemer for monetary
And other pecuniary gains.

1129. Striking A Deal

You must be very smart and pragmatically proactive.
You must have it in mind that the person
With whom you are dealing is scheming

To outsmart you and have the best of you.
Try to circumvent any dubious move,
If need be seek for advice from a trusted friend
Otherwise you find yourself on the losing side.

1130. The Giant White Apartheid

Rampaging the native land of the gods,
From its lair in Pretoria to Soweto
And other towns,
Maiming and killing the legitimate owners
Of the rainbow country.
Their cries of anguish were heard in every corner
Of Africa and beyond.
When the gods of the native land said
Enough is enough the giant white Apartheid
slipped on the blood of the innocent men,
Women and children and fell
Never to rise again.

1131. Political Party Corpse.

When a political party digs its grave
In its first term of governance and the people
Refuse to bury it they have no right
To complain about the smell of its decaying
Remains.

1132. "King Of Kings".

In order that the words of the Scriptures
Should come to pass the centurion
At the crucifixion refused to change what
Had been written,
Saying: "What is written is written".
They made for Him a crown of torn
Signifying the symbol of His glory,

For He owns the Universe!

1133. Intricacies Of Creation

Will forever confound the human brain
Probe deep as he may to unravel
The mystery involved.
The brain that designed every creature
Is the highest intelligence.
Nothing was done by trial and error
Or left to chance,
But accomplished with meticulous artistry.
Creation is full of wonders so much so
Everything is shrouded in mystery.

1134. Father Of Politics

In Nigeria with the famous pointed whiskers
And bowtie.
Not many of us knew him personally
But we heard of his political and nationalist
Larger-than-life status.
He was a pioneer of politics in Nigeria,
Whose political activities opened the eyes
Of his compatriots that the white skin
Is a mere skin-deep.
He made his compatriots drop their inferiority garment.
A pioneer of his country's political emancipation
To self determination.
Go to Sabo area in Yaba,
Lagos and you see his statue facing a popular street
Named after him - Herbert Macaulay.

1135. From Slavery To Bishop,

One of the pioneers who brought Christianity
To his fatherland.

He was a promising boy, I understand his root
Was Iseyin town in the then Western Region of Nigeria
And taken a slave to the land of the whiteman
Across the seas.
He came back a young man with some other Creole
When slavery was abolished (March 25, 1807),
And were settled in Freetown, Sierra Leone
And Abeokuta Nigeria respectively.
He started evangelical work
With some of his colleagues and established
Missionary schools
To bring knowledge and enlightenment in the land.
He became perhaps the first black bishop
In Africa.
It seems he was not given enough place
Of honour he deserved in history.
His name was Samuel Ajayi Crowther.

1136. On A Suicidal Mission

For any group of people or countries
To even contemplate any idea of another world war.
Such idea amounts to a self-suicidal mission.
In the present world of "Reason and Enlightenment"
Sanity ought to prevail in the minds of men.
The present world has gone beyond primordial way
Of reasoning, and all should key in.

1137. An Inspirational Torch

Does not shine its light into a dull mind
Which is locked against profitable ideas.
It is only a brilliant mind inspiration will ignite
To write on issues of profound intelligence
And nudge to perform exceptional feats.

1138. The Motley Crew Of Evil

Perpetrators make life crooked and unbearable
For the inhabitants of the world.
These devil's disciples live in his kingdom
From where they come prowling and stalking
Their prey in all the nooks and crannies
Of the world.
They do not allow the life boat sail placidly
On a calm sea
Causing havoc and sorrow.
Unfortunately for the inhabitants evils
Live with us as long as life exists.

1139. The Two Primary Needs

For all organic creatures with blood and water
Running in their veins,
More sharply so human beings,
Are food and sex.
As regards man all other things he does
Are secondary.
These two all-important ingredients of life
Are what make his existence worthwhile.
For instance what else animals do but forage
For food and mate though sometimes quarrel.

1140. Stifling Economic Growth

By the corrupt entrepreneurial public officials
In high positions to siphon the country's wealth
Into private pockets through the proceeds from
Two vital sectors are:
Petroleum and power where massive scam takes place.
The two sectors are the engine of growth
Of the country's economy.
But in the hands of those lacking progressive ideas

Through corruption will render the country poor
And will remain undeveloped.
In such a country a few privileged individuals
Are richer than the country to the detriment
Of both the country and citizens.

1141. Underrating People's Intelligence

Is a pastime game of politicians through hyperbole
Stock of lies.
It is assumed that if you are not a good liar
You cannot be a successful politician.
To an average politician mountains can be leveled
To the ground with mouth.
And sky is not so far up you cannot reach.
In fact you can put elephant in your pocket.

1142. The World's Deep Gorge

Is too deep and the bridge across it
Is very fragile and in a pall of smoke
To see clearly.
You cross with care so it does not give way
Under you or miss your steps.
You need moral wisdom and patience to cross
Over the fragile and smoke covered bridge
Across the deep gorge of the world to survive.
The world is too deep to see the bottom,
And human beings are the world!

1143. Serving Man Is Serving God.

We devote too much of our time on frivolities
In the name of serving God
instead of engaging ourselves on fruitful ventures
And still serve God.

Or better still worship Him through offer of praises
For it is God who is actually serving us.

1144. Waiting For Disaster

To happen before taking action.
Countries whose managers wait for fatal accident
To happen before doing the needful
Are nonchalant and corrupt people who do not
Value the lives of their people except their own.
The unfortunate thing is that they do not
Learn lesson from the previous disasters
To prevent others waiting to happen.
They hide their incompetence and corrupt tendency
Under lame excuse as an act of God.

1145. From Monarchy To Presidency,

French experience under democratic rule.
"I have not seen people eat from the dustbins"
The purported words by the Queen which sparked,
Among other things,
That started with the rise in the price of bread
The bloody French revolution (1789).
The king and his queen were guillotined (beheaded)
For misrule and disregard for the people's voice,
Thus done away with monarchical rule
And opted for democratic presidency.
His Prince never knew what it was to wear crown.
This is a hash lesson that can be argued
The people of that era had no precedent
To learn from.
In the modern day the power drunk rulers
Are still disobeying time honoured lessons
From history.

1146. The Land Of Rhode

Whose kinsmen and women ruled without restraint
And the indigenous owners were treated less
Than second class citizens.
Then one of their own with fellow compatriots
Said it was time to wrestle Zimbabwe
From Rhodesia so the white immigrants could
Make way for the rightful black owners.
The white immigrants were duly kicked out.
The usual story of power intoxicated ruler
Syndrome got a firm grip on the man not to
Relinquish power after outliving his usefulness.
His heroic freedom achievements had been
Discolored like lizard after excreting white
Spoils it with black on top.
For sometime now the former land of Rhodesia
Is fighting unequal battle for economic survival
Which the now at the edge of his grave man
Mr. Robert Mugabe has no solution.

1147. His Promise Of Hope

And assurance for mankind we live for.
He created us the highest species,
Though we occupy material body,
He gave us souls which are our essence
As human beings and reborn in His
Spiritual image.
He visited us to affirm we are His people
And that life does not end here.

1148. Matching Force With Force

Of the superpower nations.
The emerging of the hitherto defenseless nations
Are today acquiring stock-pile of assorted weapons

To match force with force of the superpower nations.
In modern day world of proliferation of lethal weapons
Of mass destruction common sense dictates
That large scale war is a call for doomsday
For the world.
Please stop it - NOW!
We are not here for the purpose of wiping
Ourselves out of existence.

1149. Climate Change

Is responsible for most of the occurrences
Of natural disasters.
we must gear up all our efforts for the challenge
And address its menace on human lives and properties.
Today we have more than enough of natural disaster
As a result of our unhealthy activities.
We contribute a lot to climate change
And it behooves us to find solution to minimize
Polluting our environment before the effects
Of climate change and their attendant calamities
Overwhelm the humankind and other lives.

1150. God Will Save Us,

The usual whining and wailing prayer
By my helplessly docile compatriots
Against bad treatment meted on them
By their nonchalant government.
Perhaps we have a different God from that
Of other lands whose citizens take their government
To task to get what they want.
Or we are the modern day Israelites
The beloved of God.

1151. For The Oldies.

At this advanced age I give glory to my Maker
Whenever I wake up to a new day
To find myself still alive.
Glory be to the Owner of life!
When the time comes O Lord the merciful,
Let your Holy light guide me onto the land
of the blissful rest.

1152. Oh Youths

Of my land and other lands aspire for knowledge
And wisdom as your loin-cloth to battle
The unequal challenges of life.
Use your knowledge to identify the plenty
Opportunities around you,
And wisdom to make judicious use of them
To your advantages.
Obey the laws of your Maker and your fatherland,
Starting with obeying your parents.
Take nothing for granted that things will sort
Themselves out unless you shape them
To serve your purpose.
Life tends to go the crooked way
And it is you who will set it on the
Straight course in your favour.
Your patriotic motto must be:
'I must be a law abiding citizen to my fatherland
And a good ambassador to the entire world.'

1153. Moles, Their Clandestine Activities

Are in government and as well as its establishments.
Their job is to infiltrate the ranks of criminals
And other such bodies they have interest.
Moles are very prevalent in the army,
Police and other para-military establishments.

The criminals also have moles planted in government
And its organizations.
But when security organs of government use moles
To sabotage each other's activities and government
Does nothing serious about it, it will render
The government powerless.
Security organs sabotage against each other
Is always orchestrated by unpatriotic rivalry
And for personal gain.
Criminality becomes the order of the day
And the country gradually slide towards anarchy
Where law and order are thrown to the dog

1154. Life Goes Beyond Feeding

For man so his struggle is beyond surviving hunger
But to enhance his standard of living with
Other wherewithal trappings.
His additional problem is how to gain heaven
Which his religion teaches him to expect.
Or his imaginative mind tells him of another life
That exists after this present one.

1155. Time For Self-identification

Of who is who building the country
And those who are destroying it.
One sector which has been the country's cash cow
And the mainstay of the economy is being used
By a few sons and daughters of the fatherland
As their own inheritance alone to deny
The larger majority in the country.
A rational mind would think the modular refineries
Being built by the bright boys in the delta creeks
To complement the shortfall in petrol
And other by-products would have been

To bring the boys on board and streamline
Their operations instead of destroying them.
I suspect the motive behind the huge amount
Spent yearly on the moribund refineries
In the name of turn around maintenance.
The aim is to sustain the shortfall for industrial
And domestic use so the humongous scam
In the petroleum sector continues.
I stand to be corrected if somebody proffers
Better argument.
Since we all have a stake with fate
Our conscience shall judge us for the role
We play individually in building the country
Of our forefathers or destroying it.

1156. Mediocrity Rules Over Intellect

At the expense of wisdom and uprightness
In a country where only fraudulent people get
What they want.
It is not an ideal country for people
Who try their honest best to excel
But are frustrated for lack of exposure
In a decadent society.
A country where your best is not appreciated
And prejudged without title and money
As back up.
In the end your best is not given a chance
To succeed.

1157. Tomorrow Will Be Good

Let us give them another chance.
This will be a continuous pattern till we miss
The golden chance to be a progressive country.
We are worse off today than the days of

"I have not seen people eat from the dustbins"
That ignited the fire of the bloody French revolution.
We are a people caught in a marshy ground
Of unconducive condition because there is
A serious deficiency of everything that makes
Business to thrive.
What could cause a serious trouble for government
In other lands is used here by our political chess masters
To capture the people blind loyalty.
The country should not be put in a position
Of a sluggish traveler who trailed behind others
To a promised land of hope and progress.
But getting to a bend of the road lost sight
Of the other travelers and could not find
The right direction to the promised land.

1158. "Pray For Your Leaders",

The Holy Bible is quoted to say
So the leaders could remember their subjects.
From my experience it seems neither prayer
Nor curse can change the mindset of our leaders
To do things that are right.
They might remember a few well-connected individuals,
The overall majority poor are always forgotten.

1159. Seamless Handover

The baton of governance is not the practice
Of our political leaders as it is done
In saner societies.
Here the outgoing government on handing over
Either hide vital but incriminating document
Or when done the incoming government treats it
With the usual nonchalant attitude.
This is happening because their aim in government

Is not for the overall interest of the country
Or the people but for their own personal
Interest only.
Such oversight can put a country and the citizens
In serious trouble like the huge sum of money
Awarded against Nigeria by a London court
For a contract default.

1160. The Gallant Soldier

Who fought Nigerian Biafran civil war at Ore front
Under the banner of "To keep Nigeria one
Is a task that must be done".
He was a Lt. Colonel then and fought gallantly
To fulfill the task.
As events began to unfold he became
The head of state of a united Nigeria.
He immediately set in motion provision of regular
And affordable meal for the people
Of his beloved country.
But the reactionary elements with their foreign
Collaborators were watching and unhappy
For one man calling the shots.
He made Africa the centre of his foreign
Policy which did not go down well with
Their vested interest.
One Friday morning the reactionaries knew that
He would be without mystical protection
In strict observance with the tenets of his religion.
They chose that day and struck along Marina,
Lagos the then nation's capital city,
Using their stooges in the army.
So the provider of our regular and affordable meal
Was removed.
As usual they tried to justify their action

With frivolous and untenable reasons.
We suspected they felt their interest was
At stake and under threat.
Sorrowfully we are still without regular
And affordable meal till date.
The Lagos international airport was named
In his honour

1161. **Unitary Structure,**
A stumbling block for the general who fought
The Congo civil war as a hero.
We remember his reported refrain:
'Not (bullets) for me not for my men'
As he held before him
The mystical crocodile staff to deflect
The bullets of the enemies.
In the putsch coup of January 15, 1966 he too
Was pencilled down as one of the top military brass
In the army to be eliminated but his kinsmen
Played the ethnic card to save him.
This move contributed to his assassination and
The civil war (1967-70).
As commander of the armed forces Gen. Johnson
Aguiyi Ironsi became the first military head of state.
Introduction of unitary command structure
Led to his assassination along with his host,
Colonel Adekunle Fajuyi, the military governor of then
Western Region,
Who opted to sacrifice his own life in defense
Of his guest thus gave honour to his race.
The sad side of the story is that the system
Of rule he introduced for which he died
Is still in operation today and refused
To let go by some section up north

Who were initially opposed to it
And some individuals down south who gain
From the faulty system.

1162. The Doyen of Journalism
Who died through a letter bomb,
Thus introduced a new scientific and sophisticated
Method of assassination in the land.
He was a prolific journalist and the powers
That be thought he knew too much
Of the shading deals that were going on.
For that he must go so the "sleeping dog"
Could remain undisturbed.
I heard his kinsmen wanted to cast
A charm on who might have been
Responsible but the powerful hijackers
In the land upturned the move to see
The light of the day.
So final judgment rests with the divine justice,
The final arbiter of human fate!
As Yoruba would say "Sleep well Dele Giwa!"

1163. Deluded People
Always groping for a twig of hope
To grasp hold of anytime a new jackboot
Hijacked our land in the belief good things
Would come their way only to turn out
An Eldorado.
Under a democratic dispensation, now
In civilian garb and their civilian collaborators
Are still taking us through the old and
An unending road to nowhere.

1164. Under Table Political Chess Game

Is played by top military brass,
Other arms of the armed forces and the high echelon
Of security apparatus all over the world.
They do not belong to any political party
Because law does not allow them.
They are supposed to remain neutral and apolitical.
Yet they all engage in playing politics
Under the political chess table of any party
That happens to be in power at
Any point in time.
This is very apparent in politically and democratically
Underdeveloped countries.

1165. A Crack On The Wall

In the land of the Pharaohs.
He wanted to rule with absolute power
Like his ancestors.
He forgot or refused to accept that under
Democracy power flows from the people
Unlike his ancestors who derived power
From hereditary monarchy.
For the love for trappings of power
He ignored the truism that "absolute
Power corrupts absolutely"
And that power is transient.
He elected to stay put and play the role
Of absolute king by ignoring the grumbling
Of his people until the army booted him out.
So Mubarak was forced out of his exalted 'palace'
His successor?
He was too fanatically religious and it is
Not always healthy to play politics of religion
With the people.
It seemed the Muslim Brotherhood wanted power

Mainly to confront Israel and the army didn't want that.
They were the ones to die on the battle field,
Not the Brotherhood members nor their leader.
And that sent him out of office too.

1166. Died On The "Throne"

The monarchical president who refused to quit
The stage when the ovation was yet loud.
He kept up the snile dance of the old man
With feeble steps that were no longer in tune
With the rhythms of the beat.
He remained stubbornly adamant to relinquish power
To the more agile in form and dynamic in mind
Who understood the changing tempo of today's politics.
Blinded by the moment of glory while in power
Many leaders like him fail to appreciate
Today's democratic trend of rulership.
And Robert Mugabe died on his coveted "throne "

1167. Rose From Grass To Grace,

A history of long incarceration in Apartheid jail
For a frontline freedom fighter to liberate
His fatherland under the draconian rule of the
White immigrants.
Together with compatriots and some sympathetic countries,
Especially in Africa spearheaded by Nigeria,
Fought with "tooth and nail" to bring the reign
Of terror of Apartheid down on its knees
And the Mandiba,
Nelson Mandela became the first black president
Of the rainbow nation -
A history of rise from grass to grace!
He got international accolade for bowing out
Of the stage with honour when the ovation

Was loudest.

1168. Penkele Mess,
The smallish grain of pepper that was too hot
For his political opponents to swallow.
The bold and courageous and charismatic politician
Who held in spellbound both his parliamentary
Colleagues and in opposition camp with oratory
Refrain:- "What a peculiar mess!"
The people corrupted as "Penkele mess!"
The smallish but a pragmatic and fearless politician
Who was bold enough to order his loyalist
To slap a presiding judge in court;
One man who defied 'no noise in Ikoyi order'
By the colonial masters to keep the area in seclusion,
By ordering his drummers to raise higher
The beat on their drums.
He would not allow foreigners control him
In his fatherland.
But on a Friday on his way from Ijebu Ode
He was involved in a ghastly motor accident
Which claimed his life
Through the grapevine the rumour crept out
That the accident was prearranged by his enemies
Who knew he would not insure himself
With charms in keeping with Islamic religion.
And the peppery politician,
Adegoke Adelabu of the "Penkele mess" fame
Which became a singsong: "Penkele mess,
Adegoke omo Adelabu,
Penkele mess" was no more!
He was a political general who died
On the battle field.

1169. And The Spirit Of God

Passed over in the land of the Pyramids
When pharaoh remained stubborn and adamant
Against the wish of God.
So there was wailing in every household
Mourning the death of the first born.
What lesson therein for us?
It is unhealthy to wrestle with powers
That be!

1170. The Only Institution

Working in the land of the Niger area
Is corruption which has become leprous
And has infected both the fingers and toes
of the fatherland,
His lips and eyebrows and has spread
To all parts of the body and became wrinkled.
The question now is what do we do
To restore him to health?
With sincere conscience search for a team
Of dedicated and expert healers with true
Patriotic zeal.

1171. Politicians Have No Conscience

To call them to order and caution them
When walking on the dishonest and immoral path,
Especially those in undeveloped society.
The result is that politics will always throw up
Decadent individuals who are bound to mismanage
The country's resources only for their own good.
The few good ones among the lot
Have no courage to assert their will in
The competitive race of:
“If you pursue and cannot catch him

Collect the sand of his footprint",
A Yoruba proverb says.
No wonder the man with conscience who
Founded the National Conscience Party (NCP),
A man of courage and defender of the right
Of the common man and the people's SAN,
Gani Fawehimi could not garner votes
To make him a president.
His generation was not ready for his type.

1172. Making Mistakes
Is in order but failing to learn
From the previous mistakes is the biggest
And stupid mistake.

1173. Only The Poor
Who genuinely call on God to make
Their wish come through.
The rich put trust on their wealth
To make things happen in their favour,
Though they too call on God, because
They know that hopeful possibility
Can be turned to impossibility.

1174. On The Knoll.
The cross was an ordinary traverse of wood
On which felon were nailed for committing crimes
Until the Son of God was nailed on it
To become the symbol of holiness.
So the King was crucified on the knoll
Overlooking His universe.

1175. The Devil's Dining Table.
If you do not belong to the inner circle

In politics juicy largesse will bypass you.
It means you have not cut your political tooth
To qualify you attend the midnight to wee-hours
Meetings where you can dine and wine
With the devil on his high table.
Otherwise you are just an ordinary member
Or a political dog…
Sorry I mean thug where a few bones
Can be thrown down for you.

1176. Categories Of Politics

Are two segments each on opposite poles
Of the divide.
We have political leaders and leaders in politics.
The political leaders rule through veiled coercion,
though we call them leaders.
They are in politics as easy way to market money
And earn false fame.
They are not in politics to improve the lot
of the people and progress of the country.
Leaders in politics are those who are desirous
To bequeath good Leadership quality on the people
And progress the country.
Their paramount concern is how to better the living standard
of the people and move the country forward socially
And economically.
They take security in all sectors as a matter
Of serious importance.
Their type are few and their good intentions
Are clandestinely being sabotaged by the fifth
Columnist who feel a well run country will not
Benefit their exploitative business interest
To flourish as oppose to badly run economy.

1177. When Congo Boiled

All because the foreign capitalists in Africa,
And their local collaborators were contesting
For the control of the mineral rich country.
They were uncomfortable with the economic policies
Of Mr. Patrice Lumumba,
A former post office worker who emerged
The first prime minister of the newly independent
Democratic Republic of Congo.
Therefore he must be removed.
He was accused and arrested and in chains
Was driven to enemy province of Katanga
Under the control of Mr. Moise Tshombe
One of the local lords hands in glove
Allegedly with his enemies.
Patrice Lumumba died there in unclear circumstances
Regarded as having been murdered.
The secretary general of United Nations,
Mr. Dag Hammarskjold who was running around
When the country was boiling also died
In a plane crash.
Since the alleged murder of the first prime minister,
Patrice Lumumba Congo was torn apart by
Civil war between the various interests vying
For the soul of mineral rich Congo.
Nations had to donate peace keeping troops
To quench the fire raging in the land
Of the unique and melodious music
Cherish all over the world.

1178. Status Of A Country -

A country whose government and citizens
Do not obey the laws of the land,
Where everybody does what he or she likes,

Is as good as not having laws.
The country qualifies as a banana republic.
A country that has infrastructural deficiency
And the few existing are not working properly
To create enabling condition for business to thrive,
And its institutions are mere glorified establishments
Qualifies as failed state.

1179. Dearth Of Leadership.

Leaders in politics are not politicians
But born leaders in politics.
Only a few manage to emerge because
The political space is not conducive for their emergence,
Hence there are dearth of good leadership among
The lot who pilot the ship of the country.
As long as political party is the main avenue
That produces leaders to rule a country,
Waste materials will always emerge.

1180. Born To Die,

That is why organic matter grows.
When the limit is reached all the organs
Begin to decline until inertia sets in
And the creature dies.
It is like you climb to the top
And must climb down.
It is obeying the natural law of growth
And decline.

1181. Pushed By The Devil

To carry out the bad things we do.
Therefore the devil is blamed for our actions.
Nobody has seen the devil,
Yet we live with him every day.

when we do something bad and blame devil
For it we are unknowingly referrin9
To the spirit in us that makes us do
What we do
If we deny this fact we are not true
To ourselves.

1182. Two Decades Of History,

Third attempt at democratic practice.
Record of the journey so far for a country
That acts like a blind man led by a couple
Of visionless,
Dishonest and corrupt minded guides
Who lead him round in circles
Instead of straight forward path to progress.
Their loyalty to him ends in pilfering
The alms given to him.

1183. The Shade Of Wickedness

In people is either subtle or violent in nature.
Subtly wicked people do not visibly show
Their feelings but are dangerous than the people
Who display visibly their wickedness.
The subtly wicked people have the tendency
To keep their grudge hidden
But is clandestinely translated into action.
People who display their wickedness in violent
Emotions do not have the tendency to keep
Grudge because their feelings are easily dissipated
In outburst
And goes no further beyond that boundary.

1184. Used As Chips

To play on their political chessboard.
The politicians understand our sentimental
Diversities in all our national life and use them
As our weak spots against our collective interest.
Immediately a political party takes over government
The political chess players start to fly
Different kites to engage us and draw our attention
Away from their non performance.
How do we rationalize the idea of talking about
Zoning presidency or who qualifies or does not
The very year a government assumes office
When there are still four years to go?
Gullible enough according to the expectations
Of the politicians these unproductive issues
Will be discussed throughout till another
Election time without tangible results.

1185. Who Is Minister For Corruption?

Nobody specifically but somebody generally.
The general overseer of the country's affairs
Who takes the anti corruption war into
The battle field of the opposition camp only.
Who wants the armed forces chiefs as his
Personal bodyguards,
The security apparatus to watch and wait for
His body language before the officials can act.
The general overseer who wants a rubber
Stamp parliament,
Puts the judiciary in his pocket.
And the media can watch as the watchdog
But must not bark if it sees a thing.
To cap it all the government institutions
Work at his pleasure,
And an absolute dictator is born!

1186. The Pathway Of Evolution

Began gradually with various stages of lives
From the original micro-organism.
As evolution took off from this simple
But mysterious base it left on each niche
A new product of species on its pathway up
Till the peak was reached which produced
The human species on its top notch.

1187. Struggle Between Good And Evil

Is an unfinished battle non can overcome
The other.
No force can stop it since both are permitted
By nature to coexist.
The common prey are the living creatures
As the grass that suffers under the pounding
Feet of two fighting elephants.

1188. Quarrel

Is a normal occurrence among organic creatures
That coexist and bound together in day-to-day
Social activities either between friends,
Enemies or dear ones.
After all,
According to the Bible accounts,
God and the children of Israel did quarrel
On many occasions.

1189. Day And Night

Are not accidental but a perfect arrangement
Put in place by the Mega Scientist cum Artist
Of all ages.
So that the ever busying creatures could have

Time to rest from their labour.

1190. The Glorious Days

Are gone when boys and girls belonged
To different social organizations.
These were Boys Scout,
Boys Brigade and Girls Guide where moral lessons
Were imparted into the young souls to prepare them
For future life.
Today the young souls are left to their own fate,
And as always the devil finds ready hands
As willing tools to employ.
So they are into various secret cults
That may ruin their lives and a tainted society.

1191. Deaf To Advice

Is likened to a man walking along
An unknown path in darkness.
He is sure to bump against obstacles.
"That man doesn't listen to advice"
Means he is doomed to make mistakes.
Listen to other people's advices,
Analyze and sift through them to know which
To adopt for your advantage.

1192. We All Have A Religion

We addictedly engage in on regular basis.
Some people practice religion of committing
All manner of crimes under the sun.
You may not belong to a conventional religion
Yet you have an ideology or passion
You pursue passionately or religiously.

1193. Bloated To Death

Like the mosquito that finds cheap blood to suck,
So shall be the fate of the insatiable individuals
Who find themselves in privileged positions
And take the undue opportunity to feed fat
On the people's common wealth.
Their fate shall be like the words
In the Holy Book.
If they and their children escape judgment
Their generation yet unborn shall suffer
For the sins of their forefathers.
And who knows, they could come back
As their own great grandchildren based on reincarnation.

1194. What Ailed Wacko Jacko

The mega star musician of international repute?
Was he disillusioned with life for what he did
To his God given beautiful black body
And decided to end it all?
Maybe with time the truth shall be known.
He had rivals but had no equal.
He came blazing the trail like a comet
And zoomed off too like a comet.
We can honour him no more than to say:
Adieu!
To international mega star - Michael Jackson.

1195. Racism,

Lesson to learn from God's own country.
A white man was about to hit a white woman
For sitting with two black women
In defense of racism.
One of the black women struck the white man down
Before his blow could land,

Not in defense of colour but in defense
Of comradeship and human dignity.

1196. Very Important Criminals

In my country enjoy good life than law abiding
Citizens and are free from conviction.
The thousands of inmates you see in prisons
Are strayed sheep without shepherd.

1197. Lalupon Train Accident.

How we mourned our young and promising
Undergraduates of the country's premier university,
University College,
Ibadan as it was called then.
The future hope of the country and their parents
Were more affected because they occupied
The prestigious first class coaches usually put
At the front next to the engine.
The second major train accident was on Langalanga
Bridge in the north which its casualties
Outnumbered Lalupon but not much of publicity
Because of the calibre of people involved.
Train accidents do not usually occur except
There is negligence in the maintenance of the tracks,
Even with the narrow gauge.
Ibadan as it was called then in the fifties.

1198. No Woman

In the world would have made man behave
In moderate normalcy,
His life dull and a monotonous routine
Without hassle and bustling.
His only nominal desire would have been
How to feed and clothe himself.

I want to conquer the world and reach the stars
Stem from desire to impress the opposite sex,
The main issue that makes his life meaningful.
The magnetic attraction between man and woman
Is an iron cast band.

1199. Manner Of Our Burial

Does not make us saints.
Put in beautifully decorated caskets and interred
In graves inlaid with costly stones does not
Guarantee us owners of heavenly mansions.
Just our human vanity!

1200. Signature Tune Virus

Is the illusion to stay put in power.
It bites over ambitious and greedy leaders
With delirious desire to exercise absolute power
Over their people.
Their leadership pursuit is like the proverbial:
"Dog destined to be lost will not hear
The whistle call of its owner".

1201. Feeling Nostalgia

Travelling down the memory lane of yesteryears,
And paying a visit to the good old days
Of entertainment drama.
They were days when things were really good,
Though we had nothing much they were happy days.
I remember radio drama: "Safe Journey",
On TV: "The Village Headmaster", "Cockcrow At Dawn",
"Masquerade", "Ucheku", "Samaja", etc.
I recall them to memory because they were
Expressionally unique and paraded galaxy
of impressive cast of stars.

It will be a glorious day for each of them
Still alive and us the listeners and viewers
To join the bandwagon of those who had died,
And leave history for those coming after.

1202. Nature Is Also Vulnerable

To evil influence of evil people.
Unless we want to deceive ourselves we all
Have heard and witnessed evil manipulative
Interferences in nature's work by evil people.
Are there no evidence of charmers interfering
With rainfall and also sending thunderbolts
To strike their victims?
We have heard of evil people through witchcraft
And other medium turned human babies
In the womb to something else.
All these lead to imperfection in nature!

1203. Three Celebrated Murder Cases

In the pre-independent days when rule of law
Was upheld according to its true bidding.
Today its sacred sanctity had been desecrated
And eroded by corruption.
A Muslim cleric Alfa Apalara and a maestro
Musician were both murdered in gruesome manner.
Alfa Apalara was killed by a secret cult group
At Ebute Metta Lagos alleged to be preaching
Against their activities,
Cut up the remains and dumped the pieces
In a bag into the sea.
Israel Ijemaize the maestro was killed by his
Alleged associates to use his tongue
For fetish purpose.
His body was deposited on rail line at Idioro

Near Mushin to give the impression he was killed
By train.
As was reported at the trial of Apalara murder case
One of the accused was asked:
"Jegede abo su ni?"- Jegede are you sleeping?
Oru we niwaju adajo?" - "Sleep before the judge?
This caused jocular refrain for sometime.
Another case recall to memory was that of
Sex worker simply called Esther from the then
Midwest Region.
I once saw her picture in the papers,
Very beautiful and light complexioned.
She was arraigned in court for stabbing her
Expatriate boyfriend,
A white man and a railway employee to death.
Her defense was that they had a quarrel
And he pulled a gun on her.
She threw a kitchen knife at him for self defense.
She was convicted for murder and sentenced to death
But was later commuted to life imprisonment.
After independence the sentence was reduced
To a number of years and later was granted pardon
On prerogative of mercy.
These accounts were dim and scanty memories
Of a growing boy not able to read
And had no access to the papers.
For clarity visit judicial archive.

1204. A Common Mother Tongue

Is the strongest bond that can unit people
Of different backgrounds and languages.
Indigenous people in a place are likely to accommodate
Other people from other tribes who understand
And speak their mother tongue than those who

Can only communicate through borrowed language
As a common medium of expression.
It will be very difficult for Nigeria to achieve
Unity with only English as our lingua franca.
We must develop a common language as our
Mother tongue spoken by all the federating units
To become a homogeneous people.
Otherwise our cohesive unity as one people
Will be a tall mountain to climb,
Much less getting to the top.

1205. They Eat From The Spoils:

If there is no carcass how will the vultures feed?
How many people genuinely want the country
To move forward?
The majority who are on the pedestal of poverty
But powerless to do anything.
The minority who have the power and
At the helm of affairs do not want
For their selfish interest.
Their gains accrue from the disorderly arrangement.

1206. The Preferred Race.

The Jews of old and by extension the Israelites
Regarded themselves the chosen people of God.
They were superior to other races on earth.
It was what their Judaic religion taught them
To believe helped by their prophets.
It was one of the offences they accused Jesus of,
Daring to compare and put the Gentiles (Non Jews)
On the same pedestal with them.
Though they were even before the time of Jesus
Under the Roman dominion they regarded themselves
Above the Romans.

It was a matter of God's wish.
The Romans did not attempt to interfere
With their religion as long as they obeyed
The secular laws.
The wisdom was 'do not mix religion with
The secular governance'.
If the Romans had tried to meddle with their
Religion the move would have snowballed to serious
Crises the Romans might not have been able
To manage and the consequences disastrous
Even before the eventual fall of the Roman Empire.
Till today the Jews believe they are God's
Chosen people and will remain in that deep
Rooted belief through their generations.

1207. How Would Herod Be Judged

When he ordered the killing of innocent children?
The three Magi who told him a new king
Was born in his domain had deceived him
And escaped.
And it was treason since there could be
No two kings on the throne.
So he put to death all children of that age
With hope the said child king would be
Among the lot.
Who was guilty?
Nobody!
But the circumstances of the time keeping
Faith with destiny.

1208. Oyelusi

The irrepressible armed robber who caused hyper
Sensational ripples in the country's anal of crimes.
With some of his comrades in crime they staged

The most daring armed robbery at Wahum Company Ikeja.
The operation was planned at a hotel in Bariga.
As early as 9am Oyelusi and his gang were already
At the vicinity of Wahum gate.
Immediately the bullion van arrived from the bank
Carrying workers' salaries they struck killing the
Police escort instantly.
The gateman did not help matter by not promptly
Opening the gate.
After the successful operation but with meticulous
Investigation, Oyelusi who led the gang was arrested
At his iron rods shop in Ibadan.
During interrogation it was reported in the dailies
That Oyelusi said to one of the police officers:
"People like you don't talk to me-
I gun them down".
It was said one of the gang members,
Folorunso the driver was capable to drive effortlessly
On the reverse gear for a mile.
Oyelusi and his men including Wahum gateman
Were sentenced and executed by firing squad
Under the new act of the military regime.
The new decree stated that if you carried arms
To rob you would be sentenced to face firing squad,
Whether you Kill or not.
Before execution Oyelusi 's request for a goat
Be killed for their breakfast was granted.

1209. The Anini Saga

Caught everyone and the country in the web
Of helpless surprise.
Every security agent sought for him and the
Authority was looking for him everywhere.
Was he an invisible wraith or an artful trickster?

He got everybody helplessly confused and
Rendered law enforcers frustrated.
Anini knew the movements of the law operatives
Who were after him before they started.
He was so elusive and his activities shrouded
In the realms of mystery.
If police got winds of his whereabouts and
Operation and tried to waylay him Anini was
Sure to evade them and strike elsewhere not expected.
Gen. Ibrahim Babangida Nigeria Military President at the time
Was quoted to ask one of the top police officers:
"Where is Anini?"
As usual the reign of criminal must come to
An end and law must prevail over crime.
Anini was arrested in Edo his home state.
The mystery of his invisibilities and source
of his information on police movements
Were traced to a police officer in the person
of Inspector Iyamu.
It was discovered the erstwhile bold and courageous
Anini was a coward.
Osunbor his second in command was the real
Dare-devil and the brain behind their exploits
And ready to die with a bold face like Oyelusi.
You the law official aiding and abetting
Criminality might start writing your will
Because you already started to dig your grave.
When the criminal is caught,
Which is inevitable you are caught!
If you take part in the eating of sweet potato
With the devil be ready also to eat bitter kola-nut
With him.

1210. Lest You Think

Saddam Hussein was removed from power and
Executed for stock-pilling weapons of mass destruction
He was accused of by George Bush senior despite
The report of international investigators clearing
Him of the accusation.
Saddam Hussein and his two sons were terrors
To the people of Iraq especially Kurd people.
His foreign policies were probably anti American
And other countries' interests.
As the "policeman" of the world dictating the pace
Of world's affairs America was determined to end
The evil reign of the man who was reported
To regard himself Nebuchadnezzar incarnate and
Done away with him.
It was international diplomacy because Hussein's
Reign of terror was rather injurious to the people
Of Iraq and a menace to other countries.
George Bush senior left office succeeded by his son,
George Bush junior who completed the unfinished job.
During the war which eventually ensued
His two sons who were acting as vice
To their father were killed.
Saddam Hussein was captured,
Tried and found guilty and hanged.
To prevent his loyalists worshipping his grave
He was buried in the sea.

1211. The Hard Nut Of Revolution

Demands wisdom and patience plus meticulous
Planning and bitter struggle to crack its hard nut
To get the inside pod for the eating.
Revolution struggle does not end in mere wish,
Full of rhetoric mainly.
It demands long and sustained efforts

To yield good fruits.
Most successful revolutions result in blood letting
As part of the sacrifices.
The planners must bear in mind that in every
Revolution or organization there is always
The fifth columnist.
People who are bogged down with tribal and religious
Sentiments or remember their families at home
Have a lot of impediments on their way
To sustain the push for a successful change.

1212. Between Heroism And Cowardice.

It does not take any heroism to stab somebody
In the back and cowards always do.
Heroes challenge their opponents face to face
Before they act.
While heroes confront their opponents boldly
The cowards slander them at their back.

1213. In The Hands Of Fate.

You cannot be waiting for fate to make
Good things happen in your life and neglect
What you ought to do to make it better.
It is like putting your business in the hands
Of a fraudster who might misappropriate
Your investment.

1214. "Ghana Must Go"

Had become like a popular hymn by
The citizens of the host country Nigeria.
When the economy of Ghana went into comatose
The citizens found Nigeria a ready farm to
Harvest under the protocol of Economic Community Of
West African States (ECOWAS),

And took the country by storm in the early 1980s.
They were ready to do all manner of jobs,
Dignified or menial.
Nigerians found cheap labour from their guests
And those with "hot" libido found easy and cheap
Sex for hire.
As always the romance soon got sour
And Nigerians started to complain of job loss,
Though had before now shunned.
The lesson here is that we do not value
What we regard are below our prestige until
We see other people making good use of them.
The outcry against the continuous stay in
Nigeria by Ghanaians became strident.
Government was forced to take a position.
The Ghanaians had overstayed their permit,
Therefore must go.
Their exodus exit left behind a trademark:
"Ghana must go bag"
Because of a particular type of bags
They used to carry their loads.

1215. Where Are The Musicians
Of yesteryear when "Highlife",
"Juju" and "Apala" music dominated the airwave?
I grieve for the loss of the rosy days
And remember with nostalgic feeling the queens
Of "Waaka".
It is better not to mention names,
For in doing so it will be unfair even
To omit one.
Suffice to say goodbye to good old days
And to a parade of stars of native musicians.
They were African indigenous melodies through

Which they talked to us words of wisdom,
The meaning of our lives and traditions
In their sonorous lyrics.

1216. Luck Without Brain

To manage, it is equal to ill luck.
Some people do have luck but lack brain
To properly harness and manage it
To serve their purpose.
The luck will evaporate before their face
And have nothing to hold onto.

1217. Aare Ona Kankanfo,

The war general of Yoruba land who proved
Himself a worthy leader for the post.
He fought courageously when the military boys
Who staged the January 15, 1966 coup d'état
Came calling at the government house Agodi, Ibadan.
We learned it was a fierce battle even though
The odds were heavily stacked against him.
There was no room for him to manoeuvre
And outnumbered with modern military weapons.
We heard from the grapevine that it was not
Until they were able to remove the charm ring
From his big toe before they could kill him.
So the Aare Ona Kankanfo of Yoruba land
And the then premier of Western Region,
Oladoke Akintola,
Died fighting as a hero.

1218. The Most Cherished Possession

Is happiness for he who is happy owns everything.
All our struggles to own this and that,
To be this and that is about trying to live happily.

What is the value of what we own
If they cannot give us happiness?
Loss of happiness is living in a life
Of torment.
Over ambitious by aiming for impossible things
Is one of the root causes of unhappiness.
We should try to live within our means,
For as they say:
Cut your coat according to your size".
That is try to be content with what you have
To be able to live in happiness.

1219. The Choicest Morsel.

No matter how woeful is the economy of a
Badly run country those in charge
Will continue to live fine.
They will continue to do the basic things
They use to do:
Go on overseas trips in the guise of wooing
Investors into the country to help revamp
The ailing economy,
Enjoy medical trips and some other frivolities
As screen to cover our face so we do not
See clearly their exploitative activities.
The leaders of such country have unlimited access
To choicest food and assorted drinks
On their dining tables,
While the common people go into the streets
To source for their daily fare from the dustbins.

1220. Once Bitten

Twice shy" is a great lesson from the two world
Wars all nations of today should learn from.
Germany is a great nation and the people are great

And heroes in human endeavours.
It was foolhardy to take on the whole world,
But that was caused by one man's ambition.
Adolf Hitler's ambition was to rule the world.
As always devil will find his disciples,
Even among the angels.
He and his disciples plunged Germany into
Bitter two world wars.
The Germans are astute entrepreneurs as is
Shown in their overseas business enterprises.
I have a flimsy knowledge that most of the English
Kings had German origin through Norman conquest (1066).
England was at one time or other invaded
And occupied by different nations in Europe,
Hence English language has more than one word
For almost everything meaning the same thing.

1221. Sad Immemorial

For the September 11, 2001 dramatic but sad hit
Of the twin tower buildings by terrorists
In Manhattan New York.
It was a sad day not only for America
But the entire world.
Many people from different countries died,
Many trapped inside with no avenue for escape,
Many jumped through the windows high up
To their death rather than die by fire.
According to report the tragedy could have
Been aborted but for the petty rivalries
Within the security organs who got winds
Of the attack.
They failed to share the information or act
Promptly on it by alerting the appropriate authority.
Whether this was true or not history will tell.

The sad truth was that terrorists were allowed
To have their way at the expense of the death
of thousands of innocent people.

1222. Oke-Alfa Tragedy,
May we not witness its kind again.
The bomb blasts from the dilapidated armoury,
Ikeja military barracks caught everybody unaware
Which led to the death of hundreds
Of innocent souls.
Those who were near to witness the horrific incident
Either lost emotional composure or damage to property.
Others far away but heard the sounds of the blasts
Thought perhaps war was in the offing.
One way or another everyone in Lagos suffered
A form of traumatic effect or shock while it lasted.
Those who severely borne the unforgettable
Sad experience were the families of those
Who died in the Oke-Alfa dirty canal.
The people died as a result of panic rush in attempt
To escape to the other side to safety.
The lesson from this is that in most incidents
People lose their lives unnecessarily because they allow
Panic rob them of precaution to saving their lives.
Like the Kano cinema hall tragedy for merely
Hearing "Fire" threw caution to the winds.
The people stampeded and in panic rushed en masse
To block the gates,
And many were crushed to death.
Panic rush had made many people meet
With what they were running from.
The dead of Oke-Alfa canal were given mass burial
At the site of the unfortunate incident.

1223. Prof. Ayodele Awojobi

As I remember him a mechanical engineer,
A lecturer at the University of Lagos-
A professor emeritus!
I am not qualified to eulogise him on his
Academic achievements,
I only knew of him an undaunted and
Courageous critic through media reports.
And we can count many others who wore
His shoes and ended his way.
Prof. Awojobi feared not the powers that be
And always ready to criticize government policies
He felt were anti people and against the progress
Of the country.
He was a torn in the flesh of the first republic
Government and too big a morsel in the throat
Of the authority to swallow.
They tried every trick in the book to buy
Him over such as appointing him either to head
Or a member of a committee or other.
All these could not pipe him down.
When you take on the powers that be,
Without the wherewithal to fight back,
It is always impossible to survive
As it also happened to some others after him.
Unless you throw in the towel before the
Killer punch is delivered.
It was reported that he died of a strange illness
Those of us not in the theatre of action
Did not know.
Rumour that filtered out from the grapevine
Was that he was poisoned through one of his sisters.
History had taught us repeatedly that you can only
Kill your strong opponent through his close ally.

1224. The Falkland Island War

A show of supremacy between Great Britain
And Argentina of who should have the control
Of the disputed island.
It was like the battle between David and Goliath
Except in this case Goliath had the upper hand.
Was it a case of giant swallowing the midget?
Britain won the war which lasted from April 2 - June 14, 1982.
The implied greatness attached to the opponent was
Intimidating enough for Argentina to exercise restraint
Before taking on the head-collision challenge.
of course if you have valid claim it is your
Right to defend it.
But this right of yours still calls for weighing
The odds against your chances to avoid
unnecessary waste of lives and materials.
There are two important remarks to make
About the war:
The Prince of Wales,
Charles the heir apparent to the English throne
Had to fight in that war as demanded
By the English tradition.
The English Media,
Especially the BBC was fair and magnanimously
Unbiased in its reportage.

1225. The Veil

Of mystery covers our face behind which everything
Is hidden from us.
Life is a mystery and so the world.
Search as we may we shall never understand,
The only certainty is birth and death.

1226. Micheal Imoudu,

Labour leader No.1 whose labour activities
Cannot be surpassed in the history of unionism
In Nigeria.
When we were boys at home in the forties
We used to hear people speak of him as second
In command to the great Zik of Africa.
Any time the defender of Nigerian workers
Was in his all red attire you knew he was
On the war path.
Once Imoudu thought a particular officer was not
Working for the interest of workers and resolved
That the officer must be removed he would
Not give the Railway management rest
Until his demand was met.
Government shivered when he demanded for
Fair treatment to Nigerian workers.
Most of us will remember the general strike
Of 1945 as we learned from those who were
On the field of action.
The then colonial government knew he would
Not shift ground except meet his demand.
Imoudu was characteristically impartial to the
Extent non of his children benefited from the
Scholarship awards that came through him.
A self-centred minded person would say
That was stupidity.
To his impartial mind it was the right
Judgment based on equity.
Nothing any labour leader can do today
Which can rival Imoudu's labour activities.
He actually portrayed the correct meaning
Of his name "Imoudu"-I possess (bold) heart.
He was and will remain an unbeatable distant

Runner in the race.
I heard he died at the centenarian age of 101

1227. God Created Life,

Devil created money as a means of business
Transactions.
So many people put aside the way of God
In pursuing money and opt for the way
Of the devil with profiteering spirit
To get it.

1228. Vigil

Being kept by some Christians in the night
To observe passage of time with prayers
And other devotional activities
Add nothing pious to one's religious belief.
To be vigilant is to be spiritually aware
Of what you say or do,
And mind what goes on around you
So you do not fall spiritually into temptation;
And become a victim of evil spirits.

1229. A Social Stigmatization

In marriage between educationally qualified women
And illiterate men,
In money or not,
Is just an inferiority complex perception held
By some people because of their social pride.
As we have often said love like money,
Indeed social stigmatization,
Is blind and has no tribe or religion.
Chemistry of love reacts favourably like magnet
On iron and does not recognize human prejudices.
Love falls for whosoever it is emotionally
Attracted.

1230. Bribery Rain

Is falling heavily in the land,
In which everyone is taking stigmatization bath.
Take a problem to any official to solve
His demeanor and body language bespeak
Demand for bribe.
Unless we checkmate the scourge its rainfall
Will cause an uncontrollable flood.

1231. A Flippant Word

Could be the means to save you from
Impending calamity.
If somebody known to be unserious and is not
Objective on issues warns you
Do not take the warning as the person's usual
Way of talking and trade it away with
Disdain gesture.
It maybe the way your guardian angel
Chooses to warn you through him.

1232. "A Voice In Ramah,

Rachael weeping for her children
For they are no more".
Was God paying back what He owned Egypt
For the death of their first born through Herod?
Only the divine judgment of God
Can give the right answer.

1233. Anything Is Anything -

If you promise something,
Even if it is the head of John the Baptist,
You must fulfill it.

1234. A Tangle With Death

Is when a man is so daft and loses
All sense of respect for elders is like
He is tangling with an old man standing
At the edge of his grave.
When the old man tumbles into the grave
The man will tumble with him.
We do not mean physical death
But moral death.

1235. God Is Not In Charge

Of the affairs of men seems the obvious reality
When you think of what goes on in the world.
With what all that have been happening
It seems He does not want to interfere,
Although not because He cannot.
For how can we explain the evils men
Unleash on the world with reckless abandon?

1236. Were I God

I would end the human race on earth!
Creation was a good idea which today is full
Of unsavouring woes inflicted by nature
And man.
God is not to blame but man himself,
And the unpredictabilities of life.
Does the Holy Book not tell us that God
Regretted creating man?
Unfortunately man is the world,
Without him the world does not exist.

1237. Public Disaster Management

By members of the public is done in general
Confusion approach.

There is initial confusion with everybody running
Into everybody's way,
Clapping hands on the heads and chests in frustration.
Objective reasoning gives way to panic
With no coordinated action.
By the time some form of meaningful action
Is taken the incident has gained the leeway
To escalate into a full disaster.
The disaster management officials finally arrived
The scene with the usual dearth of workable
Instruments.

1238. Lost Opportunity.

The people of old saw God face to face
And failed to recognize Him
Despite all the signs given to them.
Such an opportunity for which the people
of the present age are dying to have.

1239. Knowledge

Is likened to a peacock running ahead of us,
And we vainly trying to catch up.
Nobody can do but we can only able
To pluck few feathers off its body.

1240. His Albatross

Was Uzebba Grammer School playing field Edo State.
Air Marshall Alao had to die because
His plane was running out of aviation fuel
And could not land as he sought to do.
Students were lying face down on the open field
As they were instructed to do on hearing
The sound of an approaching plane.
The short but sad story of Air Marshal Alao's

Sacrifice to the Nigeria/Biafra civil war.
The depleted supply of aviation fuel could not take
The plane to the base and it crash-landed.

1241. A Drop Of Rain

That had turned a deluge
Is the success story of a boy who sold sweets
In the streets of Kano City.
The sweet seller boy became the foremost
Africans entrepreneurial business tycoon
And built for himself 'the largest economic empire
in Africa'.
Today Aliko Dangote's tidal waves of wealth have
Swept lucky individuals and corporate enterprises
Onto the bank of fortune river.
Aliko Dangote the erstwhile humble boy of Kano
Had become a colossal entrepreneur who sits astride
Africa's business empire.
He is a worthy son who had made Nigeria
And Africa proud.

1242. Everybody's Need

Is to have what it takes to move on
With the good things of life.
The pastor's prayer is to have more members
For his church to boost higher offering.
The medicine man prays for regular patients
And ability to cure to enhance his earning.
The trader prays for people to have money
To buy his or her ware.
The water seller knows people must come
And buy his water but prays nobody else
Is able to sink borehole as a rival.
The politician does not need prayer

But strategy to outwit his opponents to capture
The highest number of votes.
The transport owner knows he plies
Lucrative routes and regular commuters
But his concern is that the routes are not
Over crowded with rival transport.
Indeed all those engaged in providing self-sustenance
Pray for monopoly on whichever field
He or she is engaged.

1243. It Is All Vanity

To live in sins in the name of materialism.
Since it is not written in the Holy Books
That what we own in this world we shall
Take to heaven as our possessions,
Why do we condemn our souls to hell punishment
Through all manner of crimes in the name
Of material pursuit?
We should be content with the basic things
We need to live well.
There is no crime in creating wealth for our
Generations coming after us.
But to do so with the blood of innocent
Fellow human beings spells condemnation
For the beneficiaries in the long run.

1244. Credibility Of Our Senses

Minus what we call body language.
Mouth can lie;
Eyes and ear cannot.
What eyes see,
Ear hears and body language says
Depend on the credibility or otherwise
of the mouth to affirm the true position:

Either true or false.

1245. On The Basis Of Animal Kingdom

Seems the way we rule ourselves in this land.
There seems to exist no good or bad principle
To follow.
The only operating word is MIGHT to do
Whatever anybody does as a right based solely
On political and financial heavy weight.
There are rules and regulations in the statute book,
Nobody acts according to their provisions
But according to the dictate of our individual's mind.

1246. "Are You Son Of God?"

"I Am".
That was the charge against Jesus among others
(Not in verbatim quotation).
Were the Jews guilty?
Yes to an accusation that did not exist
In God's reckoning.
No when the Christ admitted it.
It was the highest crime in Jewish laws,
Equal to treason charge to unseat a democratically
Elected government or murder.
It was a serious sin to proclaim
Yourself a son of God instead ofHis servant.
If you read your Bible you will recall
That God himself addressed the people as "my servants".
And the people obediently referred to themselves
As "servants of God".
Had Jesus denied the charge they might have
Let Him be.
Perhaps the template on which God wanted
To carry out His plan.

Had there been contrary move to save Jesus
It would amount to trying to overturn God's plan
And no power could do that as Jesus Himself
Confirmed to Pontus Pilate.

1247. "It Is Finished!"

He said with a note of triumph,
For the assignment had been accomplished.
The divine deed had been done
According to the will of the Most High.
The Spirit finally took leave
Of the tortured Body,
And on the third day the Spirit resurrected
The Body to eternal life to be a symbol
Of God's visit to man.

1248. Living In Fantasy

Is the pastime of some people who daydream
Of enjoying good things of life;
Things of pleasure which cannot be within
Their reach.
They usually indulge in this blissful pastime,
Imagining enjoying delicious food and drinks,
And exciting bouts of sex with beautiful women
Or handsome men in the case of women.
While in this mood they have no time
To dwell on the woes of their lives.

1249. Where Do We Go From Here?

The popular saying runs thus:
If you want to hide something from Nigerians
Put it in a book".
My own view:
When we hear something through the media

We dissipate a lot of energy and time
On argumentative rhetoric with no coordinated action
Critics called "Fire brigade approach.
What it means is that we do not attach
Seriousness to important issues.
These lapses can contribute to the failure
Of a country and the people to miss the vital
Ingredients that make a country and people great.

1250. Order Of Creation

Began when a single dense matter was formed
Which took ages to manifest into unimaginable
Proportion before it exploded in space (A science source).
From the explosion the universe was born
Which made up the galaxies,
The planets and their satellites that consumed
Billion years to evolve.
Defying law of gravity everything is suspended in space,
Resting on nothing is the ultimate peak in scientific work.
It is a wonder of wonders.
On the earth planet an enabling and conducive
Condition to support the teeming life
That would follow was created.
These include the sun,
Air and water to fertilize the soil
So the vegetation could sprout.
Evolution of organic lives started until
The earth was teeming with all kinds
Of species from the lowest to the highest.
All are biologically interdependent being made up
Of the same matter,
Man the highest species not exempted.
And also depend on each other to survive.

It may surprise us that while animals had
Survived the earth for million years man,
By the turn of this 21st century,
Is yet to spend a quarter of a million.
Do your research to find out –
Creation in compressed form.

1251. The Crown Of England

Is too heavy for the weakly to wear,
Not in weight but in prestige.
On the head of the brave and strong
It makes he who wears it roar and fight
Like a lion.
On the head of the weakly it weighs him down
And may make the empire look like a vassal state.
However the crown has a prestigious regard about it
That makes whoever wears it a hero and earns
The respect of other nations.

1252. Three Decisive Factors

Influence the thinking minds of our people
Both high and low:
Political affiliation,
Ethnicity and religion.
Merit or demerit of issues on ground
Does not receive balance considerations,
But the pendulum always swings towards
These three directions.
All these will continue to undermine our unity.
Unless we override these parochial tendencies
With nationalist zeal we shall not be
One country and one people.

1253. The Main Engine

That activates a being or living thing
As an entity is the brain.
When there is damage to any member or part
Of the body it will render such part incapable
Of effective functioning,
Partially or totally.
But damage to the brain will reduce
The whole body of the entity into a vegetable state,
And semi-consciously alive.

1254. Death Phenomenon

Is not a painful experience to be afraid of,
All we need is prayer to be free of painful
And excruciating pre-death sickness.
Unless regretting leaving this stressful world,
Otherwise death is like going to sleep.

1255. Victims Of A Curse

From which the inhabitants suffer all forms
Of abuses.
The managers of our common farm
Are the curse of our dear country.
The curse is on our heads,
For we and not them are the victims.

1256. God Is A Nigerian

And lives in Nigeria unlike our leaders
Who rule from foreign lands.
Such is our belief in God:
A bonafide Nigerian as a Father- God!
Reason why we put all our problems
In His hands,
Including those we are suppose to solve ourselves.
What we do not know yet is in which city,

Town or village is He domicile.
God will not live in a place for its beauty
Or plain but a place with no blemish.
Until we know such a holy place in Nigeria
Before we can go directly to Him
With our problems.
What our brainwashed mentality has so far failed
To acknowledge is that if we neglect to perform
Our statuary duties as running a good government
Is concerned our prayers shall not come to pass.

1257. Three Intoxicant Possessions

If used arbitrarily and absolutely will fight you
While in the euphoria till you are consumed.
Trying to fight back is like "swimming
Against the tide".
The wise option is to surrender when you
Are yet sober.
Power will blind you seeing the deep gully
Before you till you fall in.
Position will tilt downward till you slip off
And crash.
Freedom will lead you falsely to the bank
Of river till you fall in and drown.

1258. They Use Our Money

To buy us because people in privileged positions
Understand our religious,
Ethnic and political mentality as our collective weakness.
After using their positions to steal billions from
Our common purse and arraign in court
For stealing,
Sorry the word steal is not used but misappropriate
As is too strong a term for the highly connected,
They use a fraction of the loot to buy

Some party loyalists and thugs with as little
As N200 to N500 apiece to stage protest
Against their arraignment.
Of course the arraignment is a ploy
To bring everybody concerned on board
To have a cut through legal proceeding
That ends in plea-bargaining.
All a mask over the face of the public.

1259. Until We Have True Patriots

Things will remain as they use to be,
Taking from the poor to make the rich
More comfortable.
In saner societies the rich are made
To pay heavy tax to put in place welfare
Programme for the poor.
This will not happen here because those
Who will make it possible through legislation
Are the ones with excess luggage.
We pray and hope our yet unborn generation
Will make it happen.

1260. Approaching The Terminal Point

By all the future lives of organic creatures
Is a possible reality
Unknown to man or yet to acknowledge the fact
All lives on earth are been threatened to becoming
The endangered species like some wild animals
He has been making noise about,
Thanks to his atrocities done against nature.
Man's tenure on earth is yet to attain
One quarter mark of a million years,
He has already eaten up a large part of it

For all what he has to do with land.
By the turn of one million years spent on earth
He would have so depleted the available land
For agricultural purposes to survive on.
After exhausting both land and aquatic life
Man will be left with no option but turn to
Cannibalism to prolong his miserable life.
The scenario will be worst than any deadly virus
Man has yet witnessed.
Charles Darwin and other sources predicted it
Years ago,
But none proffered possible solutions I know of.
It is not even a matter of prediction,
But following the manner man conducts
His activities and trace it into his future.
You who have enough today to fill your stomach
May scoff at this gloomy picture unrealistic
Possibility because you and I will not be around
To witness it.
Sure it may be unrealistic possibility only
If man does what is needed to do.
We are gradually but surely moving towards
The terminal point of our lives through daily
And gradual destruction of the ozone-layer
That protects the earth from the sun's harmful ray.
Man owes a duty to himself to save his world
For his continuous existence.
We need to preserve our arable land and end
Polluting the environment through toxic emission
Into the atmosphere.
The world body must preserve the Amazon
And other major forests which help convert
Carbon to oxygen.
Above all man must lower the rate of birth

To a single digit by each family unit to curtain
The ever increasing population.
This portends population explosion with no more
Room for his progeny to coexist.
This may likely result to future calamity
Man may not be able to manage due to
Lacking the means to further support lives.

1261. Corona Virus

Code-named Covid 19 is a deadly disease
Which has declared a total war on the world.
It is a war launched without pre-war controversies
And without preparation of sort.
It caught the entire world napping.
The warlord suddenly sprang into the battle field
From its lair in China with furious onslaught,
Which can be qualified in principle as
Third world war.
The war is being fought at all fronts,
In all the countries as the battle fields.
It is a war between a strange virus with
An unknown behaviour and the intelligence
Of man.
An invisible enemy versus mortal beings
Taking heavy tolls in human casualties
And forcing a total lock-down of world economy.
An official at the United Nations had described
Covid 19 the worse since world war II
In terms of high rate of human casualties.
This is going to be a unique history of the
21st century when a virus succeeded to shut
Down social and economic activities of the
Entire world.
It even regulates the way we should worship God.

Both the mighty and the lowly shiver
In fear before its menacing but silent furry.
Nobody knows the extent of it and nobody
Is capable to successfully challenge it yet.
Covid 19 has unleashed a kind of war on the
World to remind man that despite his lethal
Weapons and medicinal knowledge he is
After all a puny being before the power
Of mother nature.
Power that strikes without visible weapon
And with strange fighting tactics.
This is one disease in the modern world
Which has struck palpable fear in the heart
Of the human race.
In medieval Europe the people had at one time
Or another experienced attacks of deadly diseases
They called plagues.
With the meagre knowledge in clinical treatment
The people were able to overcome all visitations.
No matter how deadly a virus can be
It cannot be stronger than the intelligence
Of human brain to defeat.
Power of mother nature transcends the boundary
Of man's knowledge.
However,
Nature is also magnanimously merciful
To grant man exceptional knowledge to deal
And overcome obstacles that may come
His way in life no matter their complexities.
What about Acquired Immune Deficiency Syndrome [Aids]
In the seventies which was poised to wipe out
human race?
If not totally defeated yet its poisonous bites
Had considerably been blunted.

Virus will come,
Claim lives and go with the aid of vaccine.
From history generations yet unborn will
Learn what Covid 19 did to the world
And humanity.
As for the managers of the world's affairs
The salient lesson they must learn and bear
In mind is that deadly virus will always be
An occurrence of which some maybe worse
Than Covid 19.

1262. Aides To Corona Virus,

A fallout from the usual Nigerian factor
And a history of absurdities.
The aides that help the rise In casualty rate
Of the dreaded pandemic disease
Are the stay at home order and await death
By hunger or go out to meet death
At the hands of security personnel.
We have fulfilled the cross – road criteria of:
"Between the devil and the deep sea".
It is left to you to make your choice.

1263. The World Is A Theatre

Of war in which everybody is fighting
One form of battle or the other on daily basis
For survival.
Whether materially well off or not,
Full of health or not,
We are all engaged in the unending battle
Of life without total victory for the inhabitants
Of the world,
Until everyone of us is forced to quit
The battle field.

1264. Point Of Honour.

Most people are not honourable enough to stand
On point of honour and truth to defend
Institutional right when it is being trampled upon.
Instead they are ready to grab the crumbs
That will fall from the high table.
People with honour must defend the right
Of institution and not necessarily who occupies it,
For it can be your turn next.
This was what happened during the institutional fight
Between Governor Dangoje and ex Emir Sanusi 11.
The new Emir Bayero was the lucky man
Who picked the fat from the fire.

1265. Political Pyramid

From the apex occupied by the head
Of government of the ruling party
Down to the base of the whole edifice.
Immediately under the head of government
Are the governors,
Ministers and members of the parliament.
In the middle are aides,
Advisers and other appointees.
At the base is a crowd of assorted
Party members.
The ground they all stand on is the masses
Who voted the members into government
To continue looting them.

1266. The Ordinary Man,

How does he fare in his country Nigeria?
If he has something to give his fatherland
He must prepare to walk the road

Full of thorns to do it.
And to get something from the fatherland
Is an impossible mission unless he knows
An important personality.
The lot of the ordinary man in my country!

1267. Political Coven

Must be a borrowed leaf from the witch
Where the witches gather to hold
Midnight meetings to revel in the partaking
Of the blood of their victims.
In the same manner political party members
Assemble to deliberate on workable strategies
To capture the people's votes.
Every political party has its coven,
Although they do not refer to it as such
But caucus
So their activities do not appear too bizarre.
Political party that has no coven and do
Not hold the midnight to wee-hours meetings
Is yet a mushroom political party.

1268. A Mosquito

Over-sucking the blood of its victim will unable
To fly till it is crushed to death.
In like manner those holding juicy positions
In government in the land no longer fight
For survival economically.
No matter in which state their country's economy
Is they already have overloaded pockets.
What they now fight for is how to butter
Their already buttered bread on the front
And back,
Both sides and on each end.

So greedy they have to hold their bread
On the messing spot.

1269. Why Are We Here

In this beautiful panoramic world,
Yet full of stressful and ugly happenings.
There are so much ills besetting our lives
And have robbed us the joy due to us.
Why are we here at all,
And to serve what purpose?
I have been in search of a reasonable answer
In my mind and could not find any.
Perhaps the purpose is for some intelligent beings
Who are capable to appreciating the great work
Of the Almighty Power for putting in place
The boundless universe and pay Him homage.
Without the intelligent beings to appreciate
And pay Him homage for the great work
The world would have been nothing.
The intelligent human uses other organic creatures
And all the hosts as appreciations of His creative wonders .

1270. They Die In Heavens,

And now could not go there to die.
The deadly disease that would have pursued
Them there has its headquarters in these heavens.
And also placed embargo on their means
Of transportation.
Leaders in my country run to these heavens
For better healthcare built by leaders of the
Heavens so they do not die.
Yet they die and the remains brought back here
To be buried like us the mortals.
Their heavens mostly are the capital cities

Of the advanced countries.
Time will tell if our leaders will learn
Lesson from Covid 19 pandemic,
And build their own heaven in their
Own fatherland.
At least for the sake of their yet
Unborn children.

1271. Tribute To A Legal Icon

Who blazed a noble trial with indefatigable
Persistence and breaks the odds to achieve
A crowning success despite the thorns and thistles
On the path to glory.
He is indeed a legal luminary giant
Who has built for himself an enviable legacy
Of achievement.
Aare Afe Babalola (SAN) CON,
Actually fulfilled the adage:
"He came,
Saw and conquered!"
An educationist and senior advocate par excellence
Whose ambition is to impart knowledge
To his compatriots.
To us his students at secondary school level
He is a pathfinder of knowledge and a mentor.
His impetus to acquire knowledge and a burning
Desire for the emancipation of the human mind
Through educating the youths is worthy
Of emulation by all.

1272. Apostle Of Egalitarian Society

Whom everybody could see clearly would have
Lifted his country out of the crumbles of
Under development and be at peer

With other developed countries.
The agents of corruption did not want
No corruption tolerant leader occupy
The country's top seat of government
Who would block their access to the public purse.
They employed every theory of permutation
To block his chances to ascend
The presidency seat and made sure their
Surrogates were imposed on the people.
His sense of equity and sincerity,
Strict upholding of the rule of law and discipline
Played out when a member of the delegates
He led to London conference fell ill.
He requested members to contribute their
Personal money for the cost of treatment
Rather than dip hands into the public purse.
Made all the efforts to emerge president
Of Nigeria so he could replicate those good things
Available in advanced countries.
He was alleged to have said he would jail
The corrupt elements and they used it to block
His chances.
If he had not made the statement they knew
What he would do when he ascend the presidency.
Ran a free education policy at primary level,
Built the first standard stadium in the country,
The first skyscraper named Cocoa House,
Dugbe Ibadan and established television station
First in Africa.
He made the then Western Region the pace setter
Others to follow.
During the struggle for political supremacy
Between him and Chief Oladoke Akintola who
Became premier after him his daily tabloid,

The Nigerian Tribune was unbias in its reportage
To emphasize his sense of fairness.
For all that have been said about him
Those in my generation knew his name.
But for the benefit of the up-coming generation
His name was Chief Obafemi Awolowo,
The best president Nigeria was unfortunate
To miss.
The name will continue to ring bell
From generation to generation.

1273. Our Thoughts

Dictate our actions in our daily activities.
Both good and evil spirits are thoughts
In our minds.
These we translate into actions in what
We do.
The thoughts in our minds tell us do this,
Do that and either we obey depends
On our spiritual will-power.
No physical angel or devil,
Just a religious creation.
You are an angel or devil depending on
Which either of the thoughts you practicalise

1274. No Water Wasted

Because it undergoes a process of renewal
After use.
The water we use in our daily chore
Seeps into the soil and is filtered in the
Process of sinking into the earth.
If you put water in a container and dries up
It is not lost but escape in vapour into
The atmosphere to fall as dews or rain.

Except maybe a few monocles at the process
of recycling.
Deduced from common sense.

1275. Circumstances Make Change

Inevitable in life and in human activities.
We must be wary of our actions of which
We had treated in The Agents Of Change,
And also with historical illustrations.
Agents of change do not act without
Circumstantial reasons,
And it is those in position of authority
Who provide the circumstantial reasons.
To avoid repeating unpleasant history of change
Respect the views and the feelings
Of the people under your control.

1276. Tai The Great

Educationist and activist who sat astride
The high horse of activism.
His high moral and principled character
Made him walk tall even in his simple attire
of khaki shirts and shorts,
Complete with his panama kind of hat
Demonstrating the virtue of simple life.
He was once reported to have said after
The burial of his father:
"I cannot lose my father and lose my money,"
When guests were trooping back to his house
For the usual after burial feast.
It was not out of being tight-fisted but against
Bad practice as he saw it.
He forced government through legal procedure
To legalize the sale and consumption of our

Local gin (Ogogoro) by surrendering himself
Arrested for violation.
And why not if we allowed the sale
Of white man's gin and discriminate
Against our own.
I am not inspired to write about him hence
This laborious effort to justify my gratitude
To a man,
Though did not know or heard of me an
Unknown applicant yet responded to my letter
Of appeal to edit my writing.
He politely declined for his tight schedule.
How many in his high position will condescend
To stoop so low to a poor and unknown applicant?
His reply to my request was a mark of a
Man with a big heart and honourable.
The powers that be tried unsuccessfully
To stain him with the smudge of corruption
For which he had a zero tolerance.
Goodnight to a great hero: Dr. Tai Solarin.

1277. The Chain Of Life

Is never a straight line as it meanders,
And unsteady for the people of the world
To recline on it in peace and tranquility.
The same manner the rope does not make
It easy for the fowl that roosts on it.

1278. The Dogs

Are roaming freely in my country
Snatching the fattest meat and leaving only
The bones for the foxes.
No authority dares challenge them.
For both the league of dogs and those

In authority are running what Fela called:
"Paddy-paddy government,"
And belong to the same "chop i chop" club.

1279. Ripe Age

Does not signify automatic demise.
Except that the person is already standing
On the "get ready" line awaiting the lowering
Of the red flag at anytime for the take off,
Too soon for some much late for others.

1280. Abubukotan

Is a Yoruba word which stands for inexhaustible.
There was a time as some of us were told
That a whale once surfaced on Lagos beach.
We were told that everybody who could
Went there to cut pieces of meat off
Its body with knives,
Cutlasses and axes as much as one could.
It was either true or myth.
The Covid 19 fallout is equated to the Lagos
Beach whale in terms of the resultant
Corrupt avenues that were opened to those
On the field to exploit.
Those who were cutting pieces of meat
From the whale would not want it submerge
So soon.
So too the handlers of Covid 19 pandemic
Will not want it to go away in hurry.
If the analogy of whale was a myth,
Then my assertion is also a myth.

1281. Corona Virus Harvest.

Benevolent Nigerians and other nationals and

Corporate bodies donated money to fight
The pandemic disease and to cushion the effects
On the people.
Governments at the two tiers get the money,
Donors get publicity.
The pockets of government officials get heavier,
Corona virus waxes stronger.
We hear a lot of noise about those who qualify
To get what,
But we do not know the candidates
Who get what.

1282. Running Government In Their Pockets,

Africa boasts of many.
Countries whose managers are bent only on
Enriching themselves boast of moneybags
With foreign investments.
Their countries invariably remain poor
And undeveloped.

1283. Deceit For Self Gain.

They initially parade themselves staunch
Defenders of the people's rights.
Some of the critics are people with "silver spoon."
But are only pretending to stand up to fight
Against injustice on behalf of the poor
Who look up to them with hope of salvation
From the shackles of poverty
In the land of plenty.
This class of critics are those who make
Public noise to impress the people of their
Genuine patriotism and to attract the attention
Of government for carrot to be extended to them.
The foxes and jackals who understand

Their tactics woo and win them over
To their side to cease their pretentious "barking
And attacking" stance.
Under some circumstances government either applies
Coercive or palliative measure,
Depending on the strength or weakness
Of the government in power.

1284. "A Green Snake
Under the green grass" you are if you
Cannot do good in secret
But only in the open for people to see
So they can praise you.
A moment of praise is your reward,
You cannot earn blessing.
Though not that they worry about blessing or non blessing.

1285. A House In Commotion
Where the residents do not see eye to eye
Will not enjoy peace.
The house will degenerate into dilapidation.
The above analogy applies to a political party
In power whose leaders are often embroiled
In power tussle,
Though they unit in common interest.
It is the people and the country that
Suffer neglect.

1286. Creation Is A Scientific Wonder
Put in place by the Universal Creator
We call God.
All the wonderful things,
All the mysterious way He put them together
Have no religious connotations.

The Universal Creator is the source of science,
Hence He is universal Mega Scientist of all ages.
Man has so far only been able to tap
Infinitesimal fraction from the pool of science.
Man created religion and credited it to God
As a special gift he claimed God bequeathed
On him.
So he put the Universal Creator at the apex
Of his creation worthy of worship.
He went further to establish politics as a
Platform through which he can manipulate
His fellow man,
Using religion as a ploy to awe and suppress
Him under his rule.
It is evidently clear in all created things
That the Universal Scientist of creation
Has nothing to do with religion let alone
Establishing it for man.
Creation is undeniably a scientific product
Which its continuity rests on the pillar
Of universal science.

1287. You Are My Brother

And sister only when we meet in diaspora.
We greet and hug each other though we
May be communicating in borrowed language.
Back home in Africa we become strangers
To each other.
We hate and subject each other to ill-treatment,
Even as worse as xenophobia.
We learned from our ancestors that we were
True brothers and sisters before we were introduced
To the ways of the white man,
Embraced his culture in preference to our own.

Yet we neither truly practice his culture
Nor our own.

1288. "Operation Thunderbolt"

Truly ran according to its code-name.
Uganda people saw a flash of lightning,
Heard the rumbling of thunder and before
They knew it its bolt had struck.
The Israeli force had arrived in the night and
Caught Uganda security personnel "pants down".
The rescue operation by the Israeli defense
Air Force commando was a successful
Counter-terrorists operation at Kampala-Entebbe
International Airport in Uganda on July 4, 1976
Of which 102 hostages of the 106 were rescued
With only commander of the strike force
Reported killed.
A quarter of Uganda's Air Force destroyed under
The very claws of the strongman of Uganda,
The self-made Field Marshall Idi Amin.
He was said to be a high-handed maxim
And dictator.
Rumour had it that he fed on human flesh,
Though that could be "giving a dog bad name
In order to hang it".
The rescue operation was meticulously planned
And executed with bold approach and precision.
The then Israeli Prime Minister Moshe Dayan
Who spotted a black eye patch seemed to express
Israeli's war mongering philosophy during Israel
And Egypt war when he was quoted to say
“One eye for war one eye for peace".
Whatever Israel believe in they pursue with
Dogged persistence to a logical conclusion.

They defend their own with passion
And patriotism,
Also do not instigate fight unless provoked.
Israel seems to have a lot of influence in America,
Vis-avis the Western world.
America policy towards Israel suggests that of
“A beloved son who can do no wrong"
And by extension the Jews.
Internationally Israel seems to be seen playing
The role model race.
Israel decided to call the bluff of the arrogant
Ruler of Uganda after a diplomatic resolution
Might have been made and flopped.
Israel staged a most daring operation in
A movie-style drama.
The qualities of a people whom the Bible
Described "God's own anointed people"
Though debatable depending exclusively
On individual perception,
And swayed by one’s staunch belief in the Bible.
The truth is that the people take the state's
Assignments with patriotic zeal.
Countries whose citizens are dedicated and patriotic
To their fatherland and divorce themselves from
The self-centred attitude will progress
And earn the respect of other countries.

1289. The Impediment

To smooth legislative duties of members in our
Parliament is the single minded approach to matters
Of importance to the people and the country
As a whole.
Debating on matters of national importance members'
First consideration is what is in it for me

And what can I get out of it.
It is always me and not them.
This is why matters that will have impact
On the welfare of our people hardly
Sail through.
This self interest impedes passage of
Important legislative matters.
Every section of the federation clamours
For self actualization and has its
Representatives in both chambers.
Why then is it an up-hill task to amend clauses
Which are detrimental to the progress
of the country and the people?
Why is it so difficult to amend draconian decrees
Inserted in the people's constitution by the
Military regimes?
The overriding consideration is how will it
Benefit me?
Not as it will benefit the people.
For instance the one-leg and faulty unitary
Arrangement only favours those in control
Of the country's resources.
If not what stops members to enact laws
By way of constitutional amendments
To devolve power to the federating units?
If you live in my "wasted generation",
Apology to the literary giant the Nobel laurel,
Prof. Wole Soyinka,
The modern day William Shakespeare of our generation,
And from what had been said all along
You can draw your own conclusions.

1290. Roll-call

For those who are pulling down the country.

They are few in number but very powerful
Individuals who had held and some still hold
Or their stogies holding strategic positions.
They dictate the pace of events and their words
Are listened to with rapt attention and taken
With gospel faith by a people who had been
Subjected to mental slavery.
Only their words hold wisdom to move
The country forward.
Yet the unprogressive state of the country,
Based on their wisdom,
Remains a step forward two backward.

1291. Might, Not Rule Of Law

Is typical market-place dance of shame
By our security personnel.
A soldier kills a policeman has no case
To answer in the manner of the proverb:
"No case if king's cow eats the king's yam".
If a policeman kills or assaults a soldier
His colleagues troop out for a reprisal attack
Against any policeman they lay their hands on.
After that nothing happens except
For the scenario to repeat itself.
Nobody observes the rule of engagement
Because no government in control.
The trade-mark of animal kingdom!

1292. "Seeing Is Believing"

Is not in all cases without exception.
Example: Lion roars,
Dog barks and cock crows ,you say until
You see them before you will know what they are
Is over stretching the common saying:

"Seeing is believing".

1293. My Country Has Been Exposed

By a wicked virus and subjected her to ridicule
As a "sleeping giant".
Why would Covid 19 invade my weak and ever
Fledging country which has been unable to fly
And come of age?
The greedy and selfish managers of her wealth
Are steadily clipping off her wings through legal
And illegal massive thefts of her abundant resources
Which would have enable her soar to the pinnacle
Of her glorious nationhood.
Covid 19 ought to have spared my poor country
Now stripped of her immunity against internal
And external attacks through non availability
Of functional infrastructures.
Why could Covid 19 not borrow a leaf from
The natural disasters which take into consideration
The poor state of my country suffering dearth of
Pragmatic leadership to provide her the necessary
Wherewithal to fight back,
Indeed most countries in Africa which trudge along
Behind the giant of Africa on corruption index.
The natural disasters are not mindful to visit
Africa since the continent has her own
Home-made disasters in her style of leadership,
Leaders who lack proactive aptitude.
Therefore the natural disasters would not want
To bother themselves wasting their time when
The continent already has her own disaster
In her leaders.
Covid 19 should also have thought along this line
And spare my non proactive country from

Exposing her lacking in functional infrastructures,
Performing institutions and managerial skill.

1294. "All That Glitters

Are not gold" exhibit same characteristics
In all shades of human activities:
Presenting deceitful appearance of honesty
While the rotten inside is hidden.
A political juggernaut yet cannot carry
The people along to the destination.
Displaying a show of bravado yet no sign
of confidence people can rely on.
Very charismatic appearance outside but hollow
Inside.
Religiously pious outward but evil incarnate inside.
Angelic smile that put hope in people
But full of deceit.
Angelic appearance for people to see but inside
Is a residual filth.
Expression of love and jovial outlook
But inside is planted seed of hatred.

1295. Memory Beyond Death

From former life on earth cannot pay
Good dividends to the departed soul to wherever
Other life it had transited.
Best we are denied memories of past life
As they will only serve as sweat and bitter
Experiences which will constantly remind
The departed soul what had best be forgotten:
Best be left behind without remembrance.
As it happened from where we came here,
If at all we came from some place,
So will it naturally be over there.

We hope oblivion of past experiences is the best,
And it definitely has to be the reality
As when in dreams but unaware of the real life

1296. Two Phenomena Forces

Are the occurrences of the thunder and lightning
When blocks of ice in roiling motion strike
Against each other that produce flashes
Of light and rumbles of sound.
It is said we see light first before we hear sound.
Because light travels faster than sound-Right?
Through my observations I discover on many occasions
When there is lightning no sound accomplices it,
Vice visa thunder being proceeded by lightning.
My findings and the prolonged rumblings do not
Suggest blocks of ice striking against each other.
Phenomena of thunder and lightning are yet
To be comprehensively explained by science.

1297. Major Nzeogwu

Who was co-opted into the plot by virtue
of being in charge of the armoury and training
Became the arrowhead of the military putsch
Of January 15, 1966
The aim was to change the whole architectural
Structure of Nigeria State which was systematically
Developing the propensity for mismanagement
And corruption.
Major Chukwuma Kaduna Nzeogwu and his crop of
Young military officers in the rank of major
Were unhappy about the way the country was
Being run by the political leadership and some
Top brass in the army.
If all his fellow coupists were sincere and loyal

To the cause it would have been a success.
In Lagos the Prime Minister,
Alhaji Tafawa Balewa and Chief Festus Okotie -Eboh,
Finance Minister and some top military officers
Including Brigadier Ademilegun
A Yoruba top and tough military officer
Were killed.
There was a tragic incident when an officer
Of Northern extraction saw the coup plotters
Who were going to his house as one
Of those to be eliminated.
Tragic in the sense that they did not see him.
He stopped his car for a chat not knowing
Their mission.
He was instantly gunned down.
In the North Nzeogwu and his men assassinated
The premier Sir Ahmadu Bello and that of
The west counter- part Chief Oladoke Akintola,
By the strike group of Western zone.
Playing the ethnic sympathy the Igbo extraction
Led by Major Ifejuana the prime planner of the coup
And former Olympic high jump champion
Spared Chiefs Micheal Okpara and Denis Osadebe
Of the Eastern Region and Midwest respectively.
Meanwhile Chief Obafemi Awolowo was in prison,
Probably on trump-up charge of treasonable felony.
Dr. Nnamdi Azikiwe was tactfully advised to travel
Out of the country by his kinsmen.
This ethnic sympathy bungled the operation
Which led to abysmal failure.
Gen. Aguiyi Ironsi head of the army who was
Also to have been eliminated seizing the opportunity
Offered him by his kinsmen immediately took
Command at Ikeja barracks, Lagos.

In the meantime Col, Odumegwu Ojukwu
Who became the military governor of Eastern
Region began to spit fire and beating drum
Of war after the failure of peace talk between
Him and the new military head of state
The then Lt. Col. Yakubu Gowon at Aburi Ghana,
Which became a popular slogan:
“On Aburi we stand".
Among his complaints were that he was
The next senior army officer to take over
As head of state after Ironsi's assassination,
Brig. Ogundipe next in rank to Ironsi having
Chicken out and not Gowon,
And the killing of Igbo citizens in the North.
Brig.Ogundipe might have suspected,
Rightly or wrongly,
That his assumption as head of state would
Be a cosmetic exercise only to be removed
After a while possibly through assassination.
To him it was not a cause worth
Sacrificing one's life for.
Ironsi was assassinated in lbadan along with his
Host Col. Adekunle Fajuyi by Northern soldiers.
Before that Ironsi who had taken command
In the South became entangled in a supremacy
Struggle with Nzeogwu who had held on
To power in the North.
It took the intervention of the then Major Obasanjo
Who persuaded Nzeogwu to surrender after he had
Obtained assurance from Ironsi not to try the coupists.
Nzeogwu was moved to the East
And was reported killed at the war front
By the army from Nigerian side.
At the end of the day the coup did

Succeed by proxy:
It was the military that took over government.
Events that followed thereafter led to accusations
And killings that triggered the civil war.
The Northerners saw the coup as an lgbo
Agenda against them and the Yorubas.
Before and after the war coups and counter-coups
Became the order of the day to prove the saying:
“Too many hands spoilt the cooking of the pudding."
Competent or not every jack and jackal wanted
To take "a bite of the pudding" for his
Share and fame.
A stool of three legs will stand well balanced.
If one is removed how will the remaining two
Make the stool stand balance?
Up till today we are still searching for sincere
And patriotic statesmen carpenters who will work
And fix the one missing leg to the stool
So Nigeria can once more stand balanced.

1298. No Place Of Hell Fire

Anywhere except man plans to travel to the sun
Which we may assume the only real hell fire
And nobody goes there.
Hell fire is a religious gimmick to scare man
Away from sin.
What we have on earth is a hell fire
Suffer by the physical body and conscience,
Irrespective of social and financial status
of individuals.

1299. The Universe

Is a vast and limitless spread that hosts
The galaxies with their planets and satellites.

They are all suspended in space without physical
Support for the fact that they are weightless.
A marvel of creation!
Like the earth each has no up,
Down or sideways but to the objects on them
They feel standing on top facing up
No matter which way the planets turn.
Compare it with an ant on a round object.
Hold the round object high up
Wherever way you turn it the ant will
Feel still on it and facing up.
Such is our position on earth.
We cannot fall away from the earth
Because of its magnetic pull.
AS for creation nothing was physically done
But evolved through gradual process
Known as evolution.
We can observe this evolutionary process
In plants and other organic lives right
From the womb.
So it had been from the beginning.

1300. Postscript

To Approaching The Terminal Point:
The earth will lie fallow for some
Millions of years to replenish itself.
A new set of lives may thereby evolve
To repopulate it,
Including another set of human species,
Probably higher and more intelligent.

1301. The Pristine Earth

When man and beast were free to roam
Far and wide in search of food before

Man discovered the idea of tilling the ground
To grow food.
It was through observing seeds he previously
Threw on the ground germinated and brought
Forth other fruits.
Farming was thus discovered and man had
To gradually abandon his nomadic life
And settle in communities.
From here man left foraging for food
To the lower creatures who could advance no further.
It was a free world then when passport or visa
Was not a requirement to migrate wherever
He or she desired to settle.
In this general movement and spread on earth
Seeds and crops were not left out:
Through man mostly wherever he went,
Wind and river or excreta and carcass of animal.
All human species were first immigrant settlers
Before becoming owners of the place.
Abridge history of spread of lives on earth.

1302. What The World Should Know

About the true accounts of creation of things
Especially the human species -The homo-sapiens.
Physical creation of the so-called first man
By God's hands as when a potter moulds his pot
Is a religious fable.
At different passages the Bible contradicted
Its own accounts.
Examples:
The Bible accounts say it took God six days
To create the whole things but knowledge has revealed that
It took billions of years to create the universe
The earth inclusive.

Some people may argue that a day could
Mean a thousand years,
A position once held by Jehovah Witness sect
The Bible debunked this position when
In Genesis it refers to each day's work
As "the evening and morning" that marked
The end of each day.
God was said to confer with someone
Or some people to create man "in our image"
When we know God has no image as spirit.
Did Bible not also confirm God a spirit?
The serpent beguiled Eve which led to Adam
Eating the forbidden fruit of knowledge
So they would not know good and evil
First in which language was the conversation done,
Human or animal language?
Your position will be in human language because
God could do the impossible things beyond
Human understanding.
Would God put words in serpent's mouth for Eve
To disobey His order?
Certainly not.
If so we are saying it was God
Who beguiled Eve and not the serpent.
If indeed God wanted to deny man knowledge
Why then did the same God berate him in Hosea
For lack of knowledge?
After creating the so-called Adam God realized
The man needed a helper to be with him.
Thus placing God in a position of trial and error.
He accomplished in is by removing a rib
From the man to create the woman Eve.
Would God not know initially that the man
Needed a helper as He did with other creatures?

God also forbade man eating the fruit of
Life so he might not live forever.
How would living things that grow and made
Of matter would not die eating forbidden
Fruit or not?
Would God who created all things not know that?
Who were Cain referring to when he pleaded
With God to protect him against wild animals
And everyone who might kill him?
God did just that by saying ".....vengeance shall be
Taken on him seven fold....."
Do' everyone and him' not referring to human being?
Cain went to the land of Nod and married there.
If he was the only human being besides assumed
Brothers and sisters who were those he was
Afraid of and who were the Nod?
Who did he marry since it was not one
Of his sisters?
If we suggest she might be one of his sisters
Then we are amending the Bible record.
Had the Bible said Cain named the land Nod
And that he married one of his sisters
We could understand.
Creation was not achieved through verbal words
But through silent Power of nature.
Many contradictory verses we cannot cover
To prove that creation is not a religious issue.
The Bible is a veritable source of moral knowledge
But religion has no business dabbling in scientific
Subject as complex as creation.
Emergence of lives on earth was purely
Through the process of evolution.
Yogi Ramacharaka says "the first living forms
Were a lowly form of plant life,

Consisting of a single cell".
This formed the basic foundation from where
Evolution of all forms took off.
Prof. Clodd says: "……an embryo of man has
At the outset gill-like slits on each side
Of the neck like fish".
He went on to describe the various stages
The human embryo goes through in the womb
To ape-like all covered with hair before
Emerging a human being.
Which tells us we evolved from the ape.
It sounds funny and seems ridiculous,
Yet it is what is taking place in pregnancy
And germinating plant following the original pattern
Of evolution or development packaged by nature.
According to Yogi Ramacharaka we use the word
"Create" or "made" to describe creation
Whereas the exact word is "emanate" from God.
All things emanated from the Universal Spirit,
And not created or made.
This is explained further in "God In His Creation".
John Sutherland and his colleagues at Cambridge
University England described how planets
Jupiter and Saturn were responsible
For creating organic lives on earth.
If the scientific revelation is correct it means
The Creative Intelligence of God working through
His creation.
Religious creation talks of seven heavens
And what are heavens but planets.
Whereas in our galaxy alone are more than nine.
At the time religious creation was recorded
The petals of knowledge had not opened
To explain the intricacies of creation

Of life on earth.

1303. Poverty Capital

Of the world.
Do I hear correctly that my country Nigeria
Has earned herself such a notorious title
As if she has won a Nobel price?
How do the managers of her estate feel?,
Can they still have the presence of mind to junket
To other better managed countries by their peers
Instead to lock themselves indoor with "sackcloth"
Over their heads in shame?
Even I who has never left the shore
Of my bastardized country feel ashamed.
As they say in my native proverb:
"The tiny iroe bird says she is ashamed
If he who steals her eggs is not".
Why had the managers connived to pillage
Her estate only to leave her dissolute
And allowed to come to this sorrow past?
No matter how they feel destiny will hand
All those who are responsible to bring
Her down to this level,
The right judgment no man can overturn.

1304. Man's Varying Nature.

What particular condition soothes the mood
Of man that will accord with his liking?
Certainly none if it is prolonged.
His nature aches against any particular
Condition when prolonged beyond his limit.
A man waking up early every morning
To engage in a regular chore will after a while
Complain of fatigue and long for rest

From labour.
When he no longer labour but sleep till
He wakes when he likes and no more labour
But while away in idleness will complain
Of boredom and feels disillusion with life.
No particular condition suits the nature
of man when it keeps too long.

1305. A Pound Of Flesh.

In today's world of material worshipping
We no longer mind to cut a pound of flesh
Of our neighbours,
Whether our victims bleed to death or not.
To make maximum profits has so blinded us
We no longer see the golden injunction
Of the Lord's "Be your brother's keeper".

1306. Man Is The Devil.

You wake up from sleep in the morning
The first thing you see is man.
Go back to sleep.
What you see first is bad omen.
But you cannot help seeing him first
On your waking.
Anytime you wake up what you see first
And be aware of is yourself.
All evils in the world are generated
And spewed by him.
But of course,
Man is the only reasoning intelligent entity
In the world.

1307. Best Way To Hate

Your child is by loving him to condone
His bad behaviours.
Spare the cane and spoil the child,
And he will become a bad adult.
A potential criminal in the making!

1308. Too Much Injustice

Of man to his fellow man makes it
Possible and legally justifiable in my country.
For a few people in high positions earn
Fabulous salaries and allowances in millions
While the rest workforce can barely survive
On meager take home pay.
If the jobs of these highly paid people
Are so important to the progress of the country,
Though not much of progress have we witnessed,
Then let us do away with the services
Of the cleaners and such other menial jobs
And see what happens.

1309. Kudos To The Resilient Young Souls

Who have taken up the baton of light
For their long denied rights by corrupt leaders.
A struggle which started with the H-Tag:
"End SARS" protest.
They have gallantly proven their mettle
And no matter what happens, they have proven
Themselves heroes and heroines
Of their fatherland.
I am gratified to witness the struggles
By the youths of my country to liberate
Themselves from under all forms of degrading
Ill-treatments by the so-called leaders.
The youths have proved me wrong with their

Sustained struggles that they can no longer afford
To remain docile and toothless bulldogs
Which can neither bark nor bite,
And like a dormant volcano.
We hope the giant has finally woken up
To roar and devour the wreckers of her land.

1310. Our Earthly Clothe

The Bible says: "God make coats of skins,
And clothed them."
Nature's Perspective: God made coat for man
(And other organic creatures)
To wear till the day of his death.
Our skin is our natural clothing
We must leave behind to return to earth
When we are dead.
Man designed clothe when he realized the need
To protect himself from the hostile elements,
Starting with animal skin.
Did he not see the animals and birds
Were protected with hair and feathers?
God made nothing that was not natural for man
But will only create favourable weather
To preserve anything made by man as in
The case of the Israelites in the wilderness:
God gives man wisdom to do for himself
What he need to survive.

1311. Igbo President

When to be or not to be?
The accounts of events I am going to narrate
Here are from scant memories of an uninformed
And unemployed youth.
Therefore there maybe some discrepancies,

Though the main essence is suitably captured.
The genesis of the travails of Igbo people
Went beyond independence and the civil war.
Before the colonial masters finally handed over
The baton of independence on 1st October, 1960
Prominent Nigerians had actively been engaged
In political movements.
The existing three main political parties were
National Party Of Nigeria (NPN)
Led by Saudana of Sokoto Alhaji Sir Ahmadu Bello,
National Council of Nigeria and the Cameroon
(NCNC) formed by the father of politics in Nigeria,
Herbert Macaulay which its leadership fell
On his secretary,
Dr. Nnamdi Azikiwe (Zik) after the death of the pioneer politician,
And Action Group (AG) headed by Chief Obafemi Awolowo.
The three political parties were more or less
Regional in outlook than being national in activities,
Somehow NCNC seemed to have a semblance of
National spread for having firm hold in the East
And good followers in the West and Southern Cameroon.
In the pre-independent elections to the premiership
For the three regions Sir Ahamdu Bello emerged
The premier for the North,
Chiefs Michael Okpara and Obafemi Awolowo
Were elected in their respective regions.
In the build-up to the elections Dr. Nnamdi Azikiwe
Had aspired to become the premier in the West.
But he fell a victim of political manoeuver
When at the eleventh hour to the elections
Most of his NCNC members decamped to AG
With the exception of some loyal members,
Such as Alhaji Adegoke Adelabu and Kola
Zik always referred to as “my political son”.

The defections made it easy for Awolowo
To clinch the premiership.
By way of retaliation Zik formed alliance
With NPN for the general elections to elect
The first post-independent Prime Minister
For the democratic independent Nigeria.
Sir Ahmadu Bello was not interested coming to
The centre so he sent his second in command,
Alhaji Tafawa Balewa to contest for the post.
Chief Awolowo contested under the banner of AG,
And of course NCNC had no candidate since
It had formed alliance with NPN.
With this formidable opponent the flag bearer
Of AG Chief Awolowo could not win
Whether by fair play or fowl means.
Alhaji Tafawa Balewa of NPN emerged the first
Prime Minister of pre-independent Nigeria.
Dr. Nnamdi Azikiwe became Governor – General
Three years after independence as a republic
In place of the Queen of England.
Since the incident of mass defections Igbos
Have always teamed up with the North even
After what they suffered in the hands of
The Northerners and the civil war
Than with the West.
One might say it served the Yorubas right.
But the Igbos by this hard posture were doing
More harms to themselves politically rather than
Study the political terrains.
They lack team-work strategies and co-ordination.
The irony is that while the Igbos are always
Pro-North and give support to Northern candidates
As regards to presidency,
The average Northerner sees the Yorubas

As the best alternatives.
In the second republic there were much talks
About a must for an Igbo president.
When Alhaji Shehu Shagari came up as candidate
Of NPN the Igbos took a u-turn and forget about
An Igbo president and began beating drums
Of support for him,
Which he won against Chief Awolowo with
Controversial results and Chief Richard Akinjide's
Propounded two-third mathematical theory.
It was a Yoruba man who nailed the coffin
Of his kinsman's probable chance.
The way I see things with my present experience
Unless no Northerner comes up to contest and
With the support of the North can Igbo
President be assured.
My fear is that if Igbos themselves do not
Begin to fly a kite for a Northern candidate.
To confirm the above statement I heard through
Paper review programme in 2020 that an Igbo
Political leader say 2023 was not yet ripe
For an Igbo president.
You can now understand what I mean.
No doubt the Igbos are always shooting themselves
On the foot whether they accept this bitter truth
Or not.
Since the time Dr. Nnamdi Azikiwe sold Igbos
Politically to the Northerners they have remained
Their political subjects.
Another problem with them is this self-centred spirit
To monopolize everything under their control,
And tend to regard themselves superior.
A lot of us knew what they did before
And after independence.

If you were not a “kedu” man or woman
Sorry nothing for you.
A cancer most of us are still afraid of.
Nevertheless,
Igbos deserve equal rights and opportunities
As fellow citizens of a democratic republic of Nigeria.

1312. Poisonous Arrow!

The rulers in this country are fond of calling
On the youths in the land not to depend
Or wait for white collar jobs but be
Entrepreneurs and employers of labour.
A very good advice but from the wrong quarters.
In the sense that while they issue the advice
The teeming jobless youths know their own children
And wards are given the best education in the
Best schools here at home and overseas,
Juicy white collar jobs and political appointments
Are reserved for them.
They also know all governments have failed
The youths by not providing workable
Infrastructures and favourable condition
So business can thrive.
Therefore the advice is a poisonous arrow
To pierce their hearts.
Nevertheless my advice for the youths is that
No matter the depth of your grievances
You must engage the government in constructive
Manner as two wrongs will never make a right.
The political class really have impoverished
The youths but not an excuse to embark
On destruction of properties that belong
To government and private owners.
Some owners of the properties might have

Been in the same poor condition like you.
The irony and the truth you must come
To terms with is that government uses your money
And my money to repair the damaged properties,
Even made better.
Another bitter truth you must know is that
Your destructive actions thus provide an avenue
For government officials from the bottom
To the top to have their own cut.
It is one of the many corridors of corruption
Used to siphon your money and my money.
We erroneously refer to public properties
As government properties.
Public properties belong to you and I;
We vote for people as our employees to run
Them on our behalf.
You destroy them you deny yourself and I
The use of them.
The officials in government are well provided
With your money and my money to be affected negatively,
On the long run we undo ourselves,
Not government or its corrupt officials.

1313. They "killed" God

When He came as man to teach them
The right ways.
One of them was "all men are equal"
As opposed to what their religion taught them
To believe.
It was a strange and blasphemous doctrine
For them to swallow.
They did not know nobody kills God.
God chose to come through the natural process
Of birth

And decided to depart also through
The natural process of death.

1314. Senseless Equation Balancing

By a country which assigns as much as
Almost two third of her police and DSS
Personnel to guard a few VIPs in the society,
Sometimes carry purchasing bags for their wives,
While only the remaining one-third are assigned
To the teeming population of ordinary citizens.
If the figures are incorrect the synonym
Is correct.
The wisdom of a well- run country.

1315. "A lot of sparks

Without fire and "riding a bicycle on one spot
And government officials are in different direction
Doing different things" credited to Dr. Pat Utomi
To describe President Obasanjo's style of government,
The guardian of Wednesday 7th March, 2001.
Successive governments since 29th May, 1999
Have been riding in circles without straight
Forward movement up till date.

1316. Taking Antichrist Ideology

Too far vis-à-vis founders of other religions.
A white man whose nationality I did not obtain
Was once quoted with a remark: "Fucking Jesus!"
You may not believe in any religion.
You are not obliged to since you are free
To opt out just as you are free to take
Your own life.
But let be those who are.
Burning religious books or desecrating what

They stand for is a sign of insanity
And an exercise in futility.
As you burn one or more, many are printed.
You are only giving the printers more jobs
And more money.
And you a fanatic believer harm a soul
Created by the same God you think you
Are defending is ignorantly more insane.

1317. Ordeal Of The Poor

In his battle for economic survival
As the most vulnerable victim of inflation.
One thousand naira in his possession
Is a heavy denomination to hear.
He buys this *chikili* (small) thing here
And that *chikili* thing there.
The meager change left in hand
Wants to make him cry.

1318. The Reign And Death Of An Icon

Whose ambition was to put an end to the rot
Of maladministration and corruption
Which had characterized both the civilian
And military government in his country,
The former Gold Coast renamed Ghana
After independence in March 6th 1957.
Flt Lt. Jerry John Rawlings of the Ghanaian
Air Force was disillusioned and unhappy the way
Successive leaders in government were running
The gold rich country as their personal estate.
I cannot boast of an ability to trace an
Inclusive history of military incursion into
Governance in post-independent Ghana
But only to focus attention on the essence,

As has always been my culture.
To deal with the kernel of issues,
Essentially the lessons we can draw from them
And not the trash like how a man
Was born by one mother.
The first coup in Ghana sacked the government
Of Dr. Kwame Nkrumah accusing it of corruption,
The familiar story across most African countries.
It was a time Dr. Nkrumah was gravitating
Towards making himself a god-figure to be addressed
And worshipped with the title of Osagyefo,
The redeemer.
He later died in exile.
No sooner the military leaders tasted the sweetness
Of the pudding accruing to the kitchen staff
Than did they begin to help themselves liberally
To generous portions.
The coup attempt by J.J. Rawlings and his
Co-officers against the military junta failed.
Rawlings and his men were arrested
And put in detention.
But immediately another group or perhaps
Other members of the same group waiting
In the wing struck and successfully seized power
Which brought out Rawlings to head
The new military government.
This trend of seizing power will not happen
In Nigeria.
Ethnic sympathy and religious colouration
Will not allow it.
For instance,
Ethnicity does not allow Nigeria adopt an indigenous
Name and common language.
Wa – come (Yoruba)

Zo – come (Hausa)
Bia – come (Igbo)
Why could we not be able to coin both
Name and common language from WAZOBIA!
His first high point move as head of state
Was to roundup all corrupt civilian and military
Leaders who were tried and found guilty.
They were summarily executed by firing squad.
Whether you see the judgment from legally
Constituted or kangaroo court, military
Governments operate under decrees and their
Actions are not questionable.
This is why military rule is an aberration,
But those in government must watch it.
Under military regime power flows
From the barrel of gun while the power
Under democracy is through the pen,
And the rule of law – The constitution.
Military regimes do not see things
Through the lens of democracy,
So their first act on assuming power
Is to suspend the constitution.
Many corrupt leaders are basking on the popular
View that coup is no longer fashionable
In this modern day.
Of course irritating behaviours and impunities
In governance can occasion military intervention
Once in a while.
The best deterrence to military adventure
Into civilian rule is good governance.
Coup planning is not a tea party affair,
But a highly risking venture.
You do not know who might be an underground
Informer among the planners who could upset

The apple cart.
Unlike many sit tight African leaders Rawlings
Duly returned Ghana to democratic rule,
Perhaps when he felt he had cleaned the rot.
He contested for a civilian president and the
People gave him their majority votes.
As a civilian president of democratic republic
Of independent Ghana he ruled with fairness,
Equity and strict adherence to the rule of law.
As a military and civilian ruler Ghana enjoyed
Dividends of democracy.
I heard that until his death he on occasions
Control traffic on the roads.
A very significant display of selfless and patriotic
Service to his country and people.
If true how many in his position will pride
And arrogance permit do the same thing,
It was the very patriotic action of his
That inspired me to write about him.
People said our possible Rawlings was Lt. Col.
Tunde Idiagbon who never had the opportunity
Before he died through poison as was rumoured.
The template set by J.J. Rawlings for good
Governance is still being followed by successive
Government officials till date.
Unfortunately,
We heard the sad news of his death
Through the dailies of 13th November, 2020
By the dreaded Corona virus at 73 years.
A man no forces of men could do away with
Had to succumb to the cold hands of death
Through the new terror of our time
Rampaging the land of humans.
FI Lt. J.J. Rawlings was an exemplary

African leader of high qualities.
Unlike many of his peers whose main ambition
Was to use abuse of office to award themselves
The highest ranks of their professions to earn
Fat pensions and fame, he remained a flight
Lieutenant.
A mark of a hero.
It reminds us that all great men and low,
Innocent and guilty must bow out as mortal
Beings when the time is up for individual
To answer the final call to halt the journey
On the planet earth.
It could happen through any means.

1319. The Invisible Puppeteer

Which makes the leaves and the branches agitate vociferously,
And the particles develop wings to fly around
Like a puppeteer manipulating his puppets
Is the blowing wind.

1320. The Virtue Of Love

Is as bright as the moon at its zenith,
Its sweetness as tasting as honey
And its delirious effect upon whom it plights
Its troth makes life worth living.

1321. Lives Evolve Daily

Where conducive environment favours their growth.
Examples are maggots found in decayed woods
In damp places,
Which also may grow mushrooms and other fungi.
As some of us may have observed there are
Red ants which evolved in the red earth.
Dump red earth on a place,
Be it on ordinary ground or cemented,

When you put a piece of wood on it
In a few days later you notice a blanket
Of red earth built on the wood.
When the blanket of earth is broken away
A multitude of small ants are exposed
Which hitherto were not there.
You also notice that part of the wood
Had been nibbled by the ants.
Once the wood is removed the ants die.
This is nature at work building new lives
Where the right condition is available.
For centuries new bacteria and viruses continue
To evolve given the conducive environment
Under which they can thrive.
There abound irrefutable evidence that evolution
Of organic matter,
Flesh or plant does take place in the soil.
Lives seethe in rubbish dump sites
And stagnant dirty water.

1322. They Ruled The Earth

For millions of years before their eventual
Extinction from the face of the earth.
In the pristine periods of the earth
Among the animals to appear were the dinosaurs
And other mammoths which dominated the earth
With brute force for millions of years.
These wild animals became extinct millions
Of years ago before the arrival of man.
In my youth I heard once from elders,
The story how these wild and gigantic
Animals became extinct because man resorted
To destroying their eggs and young.
It was a story thriving in ignorance,

For man still had millions of years then
Ahead his emergence.
How then did man know about them
And age of existence?
Through excavations of their skeletal fossils
And his carbon dating technology.
They were animals in a general formation of birds
And egg laying like birds and reptiles.

1323. Deep Or Shallow Thought

Depends on the state of mind of individual.
My mind once asked me which to choose
Between publication of my collections
Of my moral and historical philosophies
And be president of the world.
Without hesitation I chose publication because
It is better to give knowledge to the world
Than rule the world.
But here I am when the same question
Was put to me between my work and love.
I chose love without hesitation because
Life is based on love.

1324. No Teacher

Education is dead and knowledge is lost,
And the light in the world is extinguished.
That great scientist,
The great surgeon and that erudite legal
Luminary giant and all the professionals
Cannot exist if no teacher to impart
The knowledge into their brains.
Teaching profession is the solid base on which
All other professions are built.

Remove the base the tidal waves of ignorance
Will sweep away civilization and progress.
When the important role of teaching profession
Is relegated to the background,
The thick fog of ignorance will envelope
Knowledge and the world is thrown into
Pitch darkness.
This is why God gave the world
The Great Teacher!

1325. Technology Of Some Creatures

We take for granted but source of wonder
When we consider their activities.
How do we explain the ingenuity with which
Birds build their nests,
The outside and inside walls seamless?
How the nests are cunningly shaped in such
A way water cannot enter when it rains?
Yet they have no hands but beaks.
Consider the ants and their castle-like anthills
Which contain different chambers.
Though we do not see them building the anthills,
Which takes place from the inside,
But the steady rise outwardly.
To get to the underground chambers where lives
The queen ant you have to dig deep.
It is a big and all fat worm,
And the main progenitor of the entire colony.
The night prowler rodents dig their burrows
Deep into the earth with living and storage quarters,
And emergency escape exit.
The rodents also have the sense to barricade
The passage way before you get to them.
In the process may have already escaped

Through the emergency exit.
What about the spiders' threads and webs,
And bees' honey comb?
These creatures are naturally equipped
With technological instincts.

1326. The Antichrist

We are talking about here is not the persecutor
Of the followers of the Christ.
He is the arch demon who is being expected
As was predicted to rule the world
With iron-fisted hand.
Did the like of Napoleon Bonaparte
Of France and Adolf Hitler of Germany
Fit the picture?
They both wanted to rule the world but
The world did not give them chance
To prove which to be.
In which nation the expected antichrist
Will emerge if it comes to pass in reality?
One of the third world or the superpower nations?
I am not knowledgeable on the subject,
Not even my scant knowledge from the book,
Left Behind could aid me.
Will he by diplomacy or coercion entrench
Himself in power?
Or his emergence mere speculations?
How powerful will he be and what style
Of ruler ship will he adopt to earn him
The title of antichrist or arch demon?
A dictatorial or benevolent leader?
A superman with astute knowledge in international
Politics or a diplomatic genius to qualify him to
Assume the topmost leadership of the United Nations?

A super intellect who will be able to manage
And manipulate the will of men?
A pragmatic man of wisdom to right the wrongs
Currently bedeviling the world or a deceiver
Who plays the role of a humble sheep
But a wolf in a sheep covering?
Is he going to be a pacifier or a man
To precipitate global crises?
The questions are left floating in the air
And with the passage of time the answers
Shall be blown open and wafted across
The wind for the knowledge of the world.
Should such a leader truly emerge and rule
With wisdom and humane disposition,
Branded antichrist or arch demon,
His government will stand,
If he rules with the scepter of evil
His kingdom shall fall!

1327. Complex Nature Of Man.

Does man need peace?
Yes.
Does he want it?
Not particularly.
If you think otherwise why does he not
Genuinely seek for it?
Man does not want war
But by his attitude desires fighting it.
If you are of a different opinion
Why does he continue to fight it
And daily turns out weapons of war?

1328. The Sport Of Death

Which is the delight of the Roman nobles

Of the ancient Rome.
Many of the nobles were of the royal families
And veteran warlords who owned trained slave,
As one owns racing horses,
As gladiators forced to fight in the amphitheatre
To amuse the despotic spirits of their masters.
Most of the weapons used were swords,
Forked spikes and metal mesh with which
They battled each other to death or
Mortally wounded.
Assuredly betting was involved.
With the mind of modern man you may brand
The Roman nobles and the populace who watched
The fight sadists.
You are indirectly guilty if you delight
Watching the motion pictures of the gruesome duel.

1329. Hoeing Towards Oneself

Has always been the way our public servants
We supposedly voted into power in my country
Nigeria renders their stewardship to the people.
They are hoeing into their own barn
The plenty yields in our common farm,
Leaving the public barn depleted.
In trying to justify their corrupt actions
One of the leaders once boldly with pride
Told a critic if he too would not hoe
Towards himself given the chance?
What should the electorate do at this point?
Take away the hoe from the selfish grabbers
Of our common wealth and give them tractor.
There is no way to drive tractor that will
Not move the earth forward to benefit all.
It means building strong institutions

To checkmate committing act of graft.
The question is "who bells the cat" if
The rest of us chose to adopt lukewarm
Attitude to our wellbeing?

1330. Weight And Law Of Gravity.

A living thing of light weight falls
From a considerable height,
Say the level of first floor of a house,
Will not die or sustain serious injury
In keeping with the law of gravity.
The air is capable to break its fall.
Similarly if a thing of heavy weight
Falls from the same height, it may either die
Or sustain injury as a living thing or gets
Broken as a non living thing
In likewise with the law of gravity.
In this case it is due to the fragility
Of the air being unable to bear
The excess weight.
It accelerates the speed of downward fall
Instead of diminishing it.
We are able to lift ourselves up
Or jump to an appreciable height aided by
The solar magnet in the earth's atmosphere.
We cannot do much because we are held
Down by the earth's magnetic force.
In a fiction story we are told an earthly man
Found himself landed on Mass.
Not yet attuned to the pressure he
Was thrown up merely trying to rise
From the ground to a standing position.
Air and other related elements like rain
Are within the circumference of the earth.

1331. Where Lies Thy Poison,

Oh death!
All world physicians and knowledgeable brains
In mysticism gather together to brainstorm
To find suitable sacrifice of appeasement
To ward off the menace of death.
Like in all mysteries they could not find any.
In the end man has to settle for delaying
Its inevitable occurrence as much he can
Manage it.
Except for its painful poison left behind
For the bereaved to bear else its mystery
Is a mere embellishment.
Stoppage of work by body tissues of an
Organic creatures through illness,
Old age and other accidental causes will
Result to death – permanent sleep!
Death involves no mystery but only its eerie
Nature invokes awesome feeling and loss.

1332. And God Came

To identify with man in his religious beliefs
As He had promised man in the scriptures.
He taught man the way,
The truth of life and the essence
Of good work.

1333. The Day Madness Took Over

In the land was towards noon when
The news of sudden demise of Gen. Sani Abacha
Broke out on 8 June, 1998.
He was allegedly poisoned with apples by
Two Indian ladies.

Everywhere was jubilation in the history
Of the country to rejoice at the death
Of a sitting head of government.
Not even the devil could earn such honour.
Government businesses and private enterprises
Went on compulsory holiday and public transport,
Which was nothing to write home about before,
And private were off the road.
Owners and the poor commuters alike were
Forced to trek back home,
Near or far.
Everybody was caught in the eddy of turbulent
Water of confusion and uncertainty,
Even those who did not understand what
It was all about.
The bi-goggled general was alleged
To rule with iron fisted hand,
Though the common man might not be that
Adversely affected but the few highly placed
Who usually benefit from corruptly run
Government.
Whether the government of the cat or mouse
The common man is sure to suffer neglect.
The spinning of thread of evil drama began
When the self-made military president,
The man people called the evil genius,
A Maradona after the ace Argentine football
Dribbler Diego Maradona, Gen. Ibrahim Babangida
Stepped aside under pressure from various social
And regional groups spearheaded by National
Democratic Coalition (NADECO) when by fiat
He annulled the election that scored the
Highest votes for Chief MKO Abiola who
Contested under Social Democratic Party (SDP),

One of the two political contraptions he set up.
The second being National Republican Convention (NRC).
An interim government was set up headed
By an entrepreneurial businessman,
Chief Ernest Sonekon which the bi-goggled
Gen. Sani Abacha shunted aside barely six months.
And he immediately took over as a new
Military head of state.
One man who benefited most from his death,
Before then he put in the cooler for daring
To criticize his draconian style of rule,
Was Gen. Olusegun Obasanjo (aka OBJ).
Gen. Obasanjo was always a lucky man
Who was often called upon to complete
The uncompleted jobs.
He was the General Officer Commanding (GOC) who received
The flag of surrender from the Biafra side,
Who became the next head of state as the vice
When Gen. Murtala Mohammed was assassinated.
Released from Abacha's dungeon by the powers
That be to take the place of his kinsman,
Aare Ona Kankanfo MKO Abiola who was
Denied the presidency to contest for the post.
Vote or no vote he was the anointed
And trusted son who would return power to the North.
And our OBJ duly returned power to the North.
What our bright boys up North failed to reckon with
Was his statesmanship dribbling.
He installed the gentle and ailing Alhaji Umaru Musa Yar'Adua
Whom he knew might not last his tenure
And gave him the lucky boy from Bayelsa,
Dr. Goodluck Ebele Jonathan to hold his portmanteau
In which resides the presidential power.
President Yar'Adua died in a London hospital

Which fact our Northern bright boys and
Their collaborators down South tried to hide
With all manner of political abracadabra in the
History of the country to keep his government
Going on his behalf.
But lucky Ebele Jonathan was about to repeat history
As a spare tyre to governor Diepreye Alamieyeseigha
Of Bayelsa State to a full governor.
And now a president.
They tried to snatch the portmanteau from him
As vice but the constitutional handcuff which
Handcuffed the portmanteau of governance to his
Wrist was too strong to unsnap.
And the kingmaker installed his puppet king.

1334. Honorary Doctorate Degree

Award to our VIP pets has considerably eroded
The prestige and lower the standard of its
Academic value.
Whosoever of our much rated pets that has
Undeserved opportunity to serve in our kitchen
Appropriates a sizeable chunk of our porridge
And goes to the university community and dole out
Some spoonful of the porridge and comes back
With a doctorate degree in his pocket
Or her lady handbag.
The awardee of a honorary degree should be
An individual who had performed a credible
And selfless service to the country.

1335. The Story Of 5 Fingers

Is the wisdom of our fore-fathers:
The little finger says I'm hungry.
The ring finger says let's await the return

Of our mother.
The middle finger says we go for stealing
The index finger says what if we are caught?
The thumb says I jump out.
So the thumb stands out from the rest
To be at a strategic position to make it
Possible for all the fingers hold things firmly.
The solution to subtitle No. 1052.

1336. Defending His Existence

On earth man needs a holistic approach.
Death through natural and other circumstantial causes
Notwithstanding,
The population of the human species
Is swelling at alarming rate threatening to swallow
The entire earth space.
Time man started taking comprehensive stock
Of his activities and devise far reaching means
To defending his continuous existence on earth.
Otherwise his yet to be born generations,
Of which I have been ranting about,
Will be forced to face space accommodation
Problem and still hope to feed
Over-bloated population.

1337. Big Ben

Is a virile and vibrant old man who live
In London whose health is constantly being
Kept in form by crack team of engineers
To remain in perfect working condition.
I remember in the colonial days as he chimed
Through the BBC the quarterly hour
And the hourly strokes to announce the time.
Big Ben is an ancient grandfather's clock

Which regularly strikes the hour on the dot.
I don't know the exact age of the great
Grandfather's clock.
To my youthful experience then as old as
The first day the Union Jack was uncoiled
On the soil of Niger area (1914).
Its maker may tell you far beyond
Or before that.
Around the world people check their time
For accuracy with old Big Ben.
What is special about Big Ben is that
It never fails to announce the time
And will never do.
Its life is under constant watch for prompt
Attention by a people who honour and keep
Their tradition and heritage alive.
The makers,
The British will keep old Big Ben alive
And kicking through their generations
Far flung into the dim future to continue
Striking the hourly strokes for people
Around the world set their time
With old and reliable Big Ben.
It speaks volume about people who know
The value of continuity,
For life is a chain of continuity.
With this humble tribute it is hoped
The old Big Ben will keep going.

1338. "Joe Lewis…
Don't forget your left hand!"
His wife shouted at the ring side
And Joe Lewis swung his southpaw sledge
Hammer uppercut which earned him

Many victories and his challenger lay flat
On the canvas grouping for daylight.
I was a young boy in the fifties
With no access to the news or fully
Understood the BBC news.
I had never seen a picture of him other than
He was an African/American.
Joe Lewis was a great and famous boxer
Of his generation.
My account on him are based on hear say
Though the core story is captured.
His wife might have reasoned that with
Slugging it back and forth till the end
Of the rounds her husband might not be
Able to win on points.
Boxers in the heavyweight division are
Known for knockouts.
Most cannot go the distance before they
Tired out.
A lot of the cunning boxers cash in on this
To get the better of their opponents.
Mohammed Ali used it to wear out George
Foreman during their fight in Congo kinshasha.
Ali allowed Foreman chase him around
In the ring and often paused to rest
Against the ropes while Foreman kept
Punching him with most landing on his
Hands and other spots not recognized
For point scoring.
Ali knocked out Foreman in the 8th round
As he predicted.
He knew Foreman was not used to prolong
Fight therefore could not last the distance.
Mohammed Ali was our generation Joe Lewis

Who was a legend of the noble game of pugilism.

1339. Political party pledge.

I pledge to my party and its leadership
To be absolutely faithful and loyal first
And foremost before any consideration
For the country and people.
I pledge to bear in mind that in politics
There are no permanent friends,
No permanent enemies but permanent
Interest as economic bond between
Members for our economic wellbeing.
So help me my political godfather!

1340. The Big Break and Tear

Of the one continent called Pangaea.
Was it true or a science hoax?
Science revealed that originally only a single
Continent existed at the pristine age on the
Earth when it was still young and fragile.
It was one big island in the middle
Of the expanse of a large body of water.
Apart from the scientific view we shall study
The general layout of the earth on the map
And also from the point of objective reasoning.
The first indicator is the concentration
Of the continents on one side
Of the globe.
The second is the appearance of possible
Break and tears with resultant shreds.
Science told us too that the universe itself
Was born through a big bang!
This also resulted in the formation of the galaxies,
The planets and satellites.

If all these happened why a young continent
Subjected to force of nature could not witness
Severe shock and break under pressure too.
Once in a while we have as reminders
Earthquakes in every continent.
We hope we are spared major ones
With catastrophic implication.
From both points of scientific revelations
And logical reasoning the present continents
Were born as a result of what we can call
The big breakup and tear.

1341. A Bond Of Fraternity.

Religious people and politicians have common
Way of thinking.
Unlike all other get together group
Politicians do not have real brothers and sisters
Outside their circle,
But members of their own political party.
In the same manner religious people have no
Just Christians and Muslims as brothers and sisters
Unless members of their own sect.
They will deny this yet the existing practice,
If not one openly but secretly.
Every interest group or association,
As we say "honour among the thieves"
Has a common bond of brotherly and
Sisterly fraternity.

1342. The Inside Story

Why a princess had to die
For desecrating the highly rated institution
Of English throne.

So much revered a duke who would have
Been the next king had to lose the crown
Because he refused to divorce his French
Wife a non blue blood,
But a commoner.
I do not have the necessary fact or
Authority to tell the inside story.
But to highlight the committed manner the
English people jealously keep and honour
Their traditions.
They are people who highly value
And respect their institution where
No man is above the law.
In Africa and I won't say Nigeria only,
Many money bags with strings of titles
Attach to their names and those who had
Held top position at one time or the other
Are above the law.
A lot of noise might be made when they
Misbehave and after a time everything
Becomes unwritten history.

1343. Ex Emir of Kano

Muhammadu Sanusi II is bigger and
Taller a personality to hole himself up
In an emirate.
He made history to repeat itself,
Like his uncle Sanusi the 1st.
When he was deposed by the state's emperor
Using the political machinery often under
The control of each state's emperor.
Sanusi was governor of the country's apex
Bank when he became the emir.
Those who run the affairs of the country

Were probably relieved to see his back.
A financial technocrat in his bowtie and
Bifocal glasses he was not always a “Yes” man
To the “almighties” at the top.
He introduced financial discipline into the
Country banking system during his tenure
As the helmsman of the apex bank.
Those that were financially insolvent were
Made to be swallowed by the better managed
And financially buoyant banks.
Muhammadu Sanusi was courageous in his line
Not minding whose horse was gored.
The man who dared the senate,
Stood an eyeball to eyeball and called
Their bluff.
Some critics expressed the views that his
Best constituency is the larger society where
He is well suited and the type Nigeria needs.
We hope he and other courageous compatriots
May stand up and fight in defense of the
Country’s ailing institutions as he did
When he was governor of central bank
So they can perform optimally their constitutional
Role and not subject to the whims and caprices
Of pretenders.

1344. “On A Platter Of Gold”

Was Bakassi Peninsula ceded by the judgment
Of the international arbitration court
To Cameroon.
Britain was accused by critics for not doing
Enough to help Nigeria her former colony
Win the case.
I do not see why Britain should cry more

Than the bereaved when some powerful
Individuals in charge of the country's affair
Did not sincerely seem to do much.
Bakassi was sold as a piece of merchandise
To launder personal images for international
Recognition.
Where was the place of the people of Bakassi
In the whole matter?
Did their voice not matter?
I recall they did protest and wanted
To remain Nigerians.
Perhaps we best leave matter for
The natural judgment and posterity

1345. Criticizing God's Doing

Is the height of stark madness.
It is in order to claim God did not do
All the wicked deeds credited to Him
In the Bible because human record
Can be false.
If He did all the things why did He
Change as unchangeable God?
Indeed He is unchangeable!
Does His handiwork not continue to be
As it was since the dawn of creation?
God came to the world to teach man He
Was at no time wicked as his religion
Taught him to believe.
Truly believe God did something wrong
Sounds like a proverb which says:
"carry sacrifices pass the mosque".
A man who criticizes God's doing has crossed
The insanity boundary to eternal condemnation.

1346. Hope To Reality

May not come to pass without working
For it.
Unless luck intervene to lend a helping hand.
You must have hope else life defeats you.
But do not make hope a reality by
A mere wish of the mind until
It becomes truly in reality.
It sounds like building a house
In your dream.

1347. Beyond Human Understanding

For He who could make His arrest impossible
Or blast his enemies to hell eternity.
Not only did He make Himself available
But only to display unequal mercy
And performed yet another of His healing
Miracles on one of them.
The super human endurance in the face
Of acute pain He bore,
He could deaden all pains inflicted
On Him yet did not all for the sake of
Unequal love for humanity.
Though we were told the reason behind
The supreme sacrifice, it did not make
It less beyond human understanding.

1348. His Two Curses

And their symbolic significance on
The human life.
Perhaps it was the season for the fig tree
To bear fruits but did not.
Lord Jesus might of course know this
Before they got to it.

I am speaking with authority but
I think the curse on the fig tree was
Symbolic of world leaders who let down
Their people,
Deceitful leaders who are suppose to lead
The people to the green pasture but on
The contrary to the arid land of poverty
And misery.
Somebody must fulfill the prophesy
To betray the Lord Jesus and it had
To be somebody who knew and close
To him.
Some people knew Jesus and could point
Him out.
But that would not do for those who
Wanted Him dead.
So they went for his disciple whom they
knew would cooperate for his greed.
Judas Iscariot thought nobody could take
Jesus for all his power,
By this he was measuring the Lord
In his own human standard.
Judas made the prophesy come to pass,
Otherwise the prophesy become false.
Yet Jesus cursed him.
Why?
For his greed;
So shall it be for people of greedy nature
Who must cheat their fellow men and women.

1349. Internet

Is an international wide information platform
And of a very large coverage where every-
Body can access information and air

His or her views.
Technology has indeed taken a giant leap
And put the whole world in one big
Global conference room.

1350. Unending Story Of Life

Is unfolding daily as 1 sit in front
Of my house,
My elbows on my knees and the heels of
My hands supporting my chin as I watch
The world go by.
I see many things and I hear many things
But do not know where and how to start
The story and how to end what I started.
Somehow I shall say my little bit for the
Generation coming behind to pick up
The thread of my story for their own
Generation to continue the unending story
Of life as the world goes on and on
To what end man shall never ever know.

1351. Getting Satisfaction

From the people's suffering and misery
Boosts the ego of the high and the mighty
In the society.
If you think the high and the mighty
Are only basking in the pleasure of their
Wealth you will be wrong.
Their chief pleasure lies in seeing the less
Privilege in abject poverty and misery.
People they have reduced to a state of
Mental wreck and servitude through
Denials of all the basic necessities
Which should normally by right within their reach.

The people are denied all privileges
So they remain poor to hero worship
And behold them in awesome regards.

1352. **Devil's Wisdom**
Lead to damnation and hell fire.
It is good and worthy of God's blessings
To be a fool and keep all His laws
Than to be a wise man in devil's
Kingdom.

1353. **Hope Suspended.**
It takes extraordinary miracles for a
Bad government to meet the yearning of
The people it governs.
It is a government which does not turn
The hope of the people to reality.
Through the optimism the citizens hold on
To hope which remains on indefinite
Suspension like weightless particles
Suspended in mid-air.
Even the air relents to allow the particle
Drift down onto the ground.
No our remorseless officials in
Bad government are not thinking
Of relenting.

1354. **Mobility Technology**
Now gives the man means of faster and
Without stress movement from one place
To another within the shortest time in
This modern day.
Man can now travel easily with convenience
And in comfort.

But he has to pay high price in human
Casualties and damage to properties as
Sacrifices to appease the god of technology.
Like Yoruba and some others tribes who offer
Sacrifices with dogs to ward off vehicular
Accidents.
Yoruba call it "sacrifice to god of iron".
In the olden days of our forefathers
Travelling was hazardous and somewhat
Energy sapped trekking under terrible weather,
As a result exhaustion and sometimes death may occur.

1355. Creation

Is a layman word to describe beginning
Of the universe and things.
Emanation and evolution are the right words,
Though creation is the best synonym.
Life was not created or made but
Emanated from the universal spirit – God.
In creating or making you observe action
Of building and growing stage by stage
Of the object in the making.
For example when a potter is molding
His pot you can follow the progress
Of action and its growth.
For emanation or evolving you do not see
Physical action taking place
Only the result of what emanation or
Evolution had achieved.
The work of creating is seen but that
Of evolution is not seen.
However creation or emanation had stopped
Since the birth of the universe and its host.

Evolution takes place in a mysterious manner
In the objects emanation or creation had
Succeeded to bring forth.
If it were possible to focus attention on
A shooting plant for days without blinking eyes
You cannot see stage by stage progress of building
But the result of growth.
A baby in the womb of an organic creature,
Example is that of human embryo,
Goes through different stages as we have
Earlier observed until the final stage is reached.
Life was not accidental but meticulously
Designed and executed by the universal
Intelligence !
What takes place today is evolution of
Existing life as packaged by nature.

1356. Sharing Your Wealth

Before you own it is fulfilling the proverbs:
"living in a fool's paradise",
"building a castle in the air" and
"don't count your chickens before they
Are hatched".
In my place a proverb says: "Hang your bag
On a peg within the reach of your hand".
Sharing what you are yet or expected
To own is a sign of over ambition.
Such people live a depressed life.
To have ambition is good but to be
Over ambitious is a recipe for unhappy
Life.

1357. Where Exists Heaven?

From the Bible's perspective heaven,

(or heavens) is a place where exists life
Of pleasure for the righteous soul:
That is, a state of paradise.
There is also hell where everlasting fire
Burns sinners.
Are there truly such places?
These are religious beliefs which their
Authenticity cannot be proved.
The beliefs stand to serve as promise
Of hope for those whose minds are
Amenable to righteousness and deterrence
For prospective sinners to depart their
Evil ways.
What is certain and proved by science
Are existence of planets which,
Apart from the earth,
May exist life.
For instance a science report says some
Of the planets may be good candidates
To have life because they have pork marks
Like the earth and moon.
If indeed there must be heaven or heavens
They must be some of the planets.
Besides planets nowhere else is existence
Available or possible.
The universe is all inclusive.
Whether there is a place of pleasure
Or not certainly no such a place as hell
Where sinners burn forever.
What is unprovable remains an illusion.
It has been mentioned elsewhere that here
On earth individually we do experience
Life of pleasure and also undergo a form
Of hell.

No matter how wise or inspired no man
Can give a true condition of things
In the celestial heavens-The planets.

1358. "Eesobey!"

Is a bastardize word to encourage ourselves
To put more effort on the task we are
Engaged to do.
Many people do not know the word
Or the full meaning.
When some merchant sailors,
The like of Williams Wilberforce,
Francis Drake and co during Elizabeth
The 1st era (aka Elizabethan Seadogs)
Discovered America the rich yields and minerals
They brought back from the virgin land attracted
The investors in England to invest in plantations
And prospect for minerals and oils.
Prisoners,
Felon not wanted in England and those who
Indentured themselves as labour were shipped
To the new land.
But their output was poor so the investors
Turned their attention to the "dark continent",
Africa for labour.
They got them in their numbers through
The local chiefs enticed with cheap and
Glossy articles.
Also the warlords sold their captured prisoners
To the white slave traders and their black agents.
So the Africans were as much guilty too.
Whenever the overseers felt the black slaves
Were slacking on the job,
With wipes in hands,

Would shout at them: "Apes obey!"
When slavery was abolished in 1807 who
Cared to return to their ancestral land came
Back with the bastardize version which
Became a word of encouragement in our
Vocabulary lexicon.

1359. God in His Creation.

Anything that has no element
Of God cannot exist.
God is a Universal Mega Scientist of all ages.
If you disagree tell me of one thing created
By God which is not scientific in making.
When you perform genetic cloning it is nature
Which makes the end result possible.
Man decided to worship Him through his
Religion for His great work of creation
Which remains a mystery to his scientific knowledge.
God in His creation desires and instantly
Becomes fulfilled, we call it miracle.
That was why when Jesus performed miracles
They were instantly fulfilled.

1360. Beware of Forgetfulness

As a serious deficiency in man:
A man who easily forgets things must
Always watch it and be conscious of his
Shortcoming as a reminder to avoid danger.
Else the unexpected happens.
Forgetfulness may cause you a great loss.
The only cure to forgetfulness,
Like mistake is constantly be aware
Of it and you are likely to remember.

1361. Our Currency Flight

Out of circulation is something serious
And ought to bother our policy makers
Who run the country.
It hinders smooth business transaction
And the common man is always the victim
Who cannot engage in bulk purchasing.
A corrupt government is weak and a weak
Government is corrupt.
It will be unable to enforce its policies.
A fertile ground is created for all sorts
Of impunities in running government business.
Abinitio Kobo coins did not perform at all,
And government is too weak to enforce
Its policies.
Five naira paper note was the first to go out
Of circulation after a brief performance,
Boarded the inflation jet plane and flew out.
Ten naira is warming up to take a leave
Of the country and we can now hardly see
Its back.
You buy a ten naira worth of an article
The seller does not have ten naira change
So you are forced to buy at twenty naira.
These currency notes did not actually
Fly out of the country
But their purchasing power.
The fate of twenty,
Fifty and hundred naira notes may in
Future hang in the balance where no
Effective government in control.
In countries whose leaders in government
Are serious, they do not allow the purchasing
Power of their currencies depreciate
And lose value.

Worst of all allow any denomination
Out of circulation unless through an act
Of parliament.

1362. Sharing The National Cake

Has been a battle royal since this
"Geographical expression",
Credited to the sage Chief Obafemi
Awolowo,
Called Nigeria got her independence
From her former colonial master,
The Great Britain in 1st October, 1960.
The contestants are both civilian and military
Adventurers who try to convince us that
They represent their respective regions.
They are like the fable "Fortune Hunters".
Igbos want to dominate the national life
Of the country from the top to the bottom.
Hausas/Fulanis must be the head,
From the neck down to the middle and
The lower cadre anybody can be there.
Yorubas also want to be head but
They are liberal minded and ready to
Tolerate and accommodate others.
The other ethnic groups are pushover
Except now that states have been created
For them to keep the peace.
But in the deadly fight the censor figures
Are manipulated to give false data in a bid
To have the best of the others.
How does the common man fare in sharing
Of the bounties of the giant of Africa?
The civilians and those who had shed
Their military garbs for civilian clothes

Are not giving opportunities to the
Ordinary man for equal distribution
Of services and wealth.
It is a common knowledge our so-called
Representatives and others who have
Opportunities in driving the economic vehicles
Of the country want us to know they
Are driving the economic vehicles in the
Interest of their regions and the people.
But the huge sum of money they get
Does not translate to development.
Instead it creates overnight kingpins pregnant
With cash stashed away in both local
    And foreign banks.
    The greedy mentality to grab all
    Has continued to be curse on the country
    And the ordinary man.

1363. Issues With Ground

Is another story from the stable
Of our forefathers.
Ogogo is a bird bigger than eagle.
It is not common and flies high.
It has elongated beak that terminates
On its head with hard bulge.
It says it buried its mother on its head
Because ground did not exit at the time
It arrived in the world.
Chameleon says it was shaking because
Ground on which it was standing when
It arrived in the world was weak
And still shaking.
Praying Mantis says it constantly pray
So the ground does not cave in under it.

1364. Honourable Members,

A code of conduct for all the world's
Parliamentarians.
A revisit to "The Noble Tradition" of my people
When the Chiefs and age grades are holding
Meetings.
Proceedings are conducted in an atmosphere
Of cordiality,
Contributions based on points without
Rancor and abusive words.
The decorum and discipline of civilized
Culture of handling issues display maturity.
Yet their forebear who laid down the
Noble tradition principle of interactions
Were not exposed to Western education.
There is no written rules to guide proceedings
But traditional rules written in mind.
Perhaps many never heard of Britain
But here unknowingly adopted home grown
Magna Carta.
The noble tradition.
When a speaker ends his speech the chairman
Or who heads the meeting will intone:
"Well spoken or you have spoken well!"
A member may not say anything with
Much sense but as long as he does not
Use abusive words in his speech
He gets the commendation.
The views of the contributors members
Will consider to arrive on a general consensus.
No arguments no abuses.
Men with clear conscience had spoken
Their minds for the progress of their

Community and decisions taken.

1365. Operation Wetie

Wetie was a conjoined English and Yoruba word,
Meaning wet it.
It was coined during the aftermath of premiership elections
Between Chief Obafemi Awolowo and Chief Oladoke Akintola,
Of Western Region in 1964.
Both Awolowo and Akintola were members of
Action Group (AG) as leaders with its machinery
Under the control of Chief Awolowo.
Political relevance and power tussle made Chief Akintola
Break away and formed a parallel political party,
Democratic Alliance and teamed up with
National Party of Nigeria (NPN).
This move made his opponents brand him a
Northern surrogate which gave birth to a Yoruba
Singsong refrain: "Demo ni mo wa,
Bo rowo mi o ri' ku mi demo ni mo wa".
Meaning "I'm for demo,
If you see my hands you don't see my belly".
Immediately after the end of the elections rumours became rife
That Chief Akintola was in the lead.
Loyalists of Chief Awolowo were alleging that
Their leader was shortchanged and was rigged out.
There and then devil was let loose to roam
Freely untamed.
Houses and properties belonging to perceived members
Of the opposition camp were visited with arson.
Properties and even sometimes human beings were
Doused with petrol and set on fire.
The day was turned "a red – letter day" as they say it.
By the second day a new dimension was introduced.
It quickly developed as means of making easy

Money and owners of sudden properties.
It no longer count whether you belong to a
Political party or not.
The only acceptable political party was money or
Valuable items.
As it turned out an opportunity for miscreants
To ply their trade, hijacked operation wetie.
They came to your house and were happy you
Knew some of them who would bail you out meant
You were hoping for "a fool's paradise".
It was money or valuable items that would open
Their eyes to recognize you.
They will tell you knowing you made it possible
To accept your money or something instead of
Burning your house or even you.
A diabolical new invention in the realm of black
Scientific aspect was added.
It said they set things or human beings on fire
By merely throwing raw eggs on the objects
And instantly fire would occur.
I did not witness any and I did not see
Actual burning of anything.
But I saw many burnt houses and cars.
The whole scenario had assumed a dangerous scale.
It was compared to American Texas's "Wild Wild West".
The role of the police in all these?
They were simply overwhelmed but must show
They were trying their best to restore peace.
The police would come rushing to the place where
A house was burnt hours after the perpetrators
Had gone and arrested whosoever were unlucky
To pass through the area.
They must make arrest if not to punish
But earn bail money.

In the end Chief Oladoke Akintola was declared
Winner of the premiership election.
The crises in the Wild Wild West contributed
Directly or indirectly to taking over government
At the centre and the civil war.

1366. A Poisoned Mind

Belongs to a man who cannot truly be
"His brother's keeper" to his neighbours.
To be that he has to sacrifice his poisoned
Mind on the altar of good neighbourness
And adhere to all the moral virtues
If he desires to see the face of God.

1367. Obligatory Services

Are what our public servants render
To the members of the public and government
As though they are not their constitutional
Responsibilities.
They feel they owe us no allegiance even
As they are paid with our taxpayer's money.
The civil servants' jobs run or rather
Crawl in a snail pace slithering motion
That promises no progress.
Government is not the loser nor its
Corrupt officials who make use of the
Civil servants services for their own
Personal shady deals.
It is the common citizens and the country
Who suffer their unprogressive services.

1368. Trust Based On Religion

By anybody may have fallen into deep pit
Before realizing it.

This position is not to say there are no
Honest and trusting minds among religious
Practitioners.
The fact is that our behaviours come
From the mind controlled by instincts
Than what we meet and acquire here.
Religion or tradition,
Even our acquired knowledge,
Can only help mend our natural behaviours
If bad or enhance them if good.

1369. Straight Arrow

From an expert archer goes directly
To hit the target.
This is how we describe people who are
Very strict and uncompromising in their
Words and actions.
When they target something they hardly let go
Not until they have seen the front and back of it.
In their hardliner posture they hardly
Shift position – sweet or bitter.
They are not necessarily wicked,
Just being disciplinarians by nature.
They say it as it is and want it done
As it should, not minding "whose horse is gored".
They do not compromise their stand
To giving or receiving bribe.

1370. Ovbudu A King–pin Thief

Hailed from Avbiosi a sister town to Uzebba in
Owan west local government area of Edo state, Nigeria.
He was a notorious thief known even to
The little children who hardly knew anything.
There was a time he was been chased and ran

Past our backyard into the bush where he was captured.
What I would not connect now is whether the arrest
Had to do with the accounts I am going
To give about him.
Related or not all was about him.
Izodu (not real name) had made his life in a
Big city probably Ibadan.
He had returned to his hometown Uzebba
And on the sideline sometimes went for hunting,
He was returning early in the morning in one of the outings
When he met Ovbudu and his gang members.
They were returning from stealing escapade.
As friends perhaps Izodu advised him to give up
That kind of occupation and find a legal means
To earn a living.
With that they went their separate ways.
But then that ever present demon in human mind
Sowed the evil seed in their minds that the man
Would tell on them.
They went back after Izodu and before he knew
What was going to happen to him they started
To machete him till he was dead.
Advised them or not that same evil thought
Would still urge them to kill him.
As usual in criminality no matter how meticulously
The criminals tried to block all loopholes they are
Bound to omit one law will exploit to catch them.
Izodu was not yet quite dead before early morning
Risers who were going about their duties found him
And was able to breathe out the name 'Ovbudu'.
Ovbudu and his gang members were arrested
In his hometown Avbiosi.
They were stripped of clothing except their short pants
Before their arms were tied to the back with cords

From their wrists to elbow joints.
The tied arms were occasionally sprinkled with water,
Though at the time I did not know why.
It was a frightening entertainment to us children.
I did not know what happened after,
Probably sentenced to death for stealing and murder
Or least life imprisonment.
I did not hear anything about him again till
I was taken to Ibadan where I started schooling
At the age of about 14 years old.
Why I narrate the story is to show that in
Every society civilized or primitive you find
The same behaviours unless it is not human beings
Who inhabit the place.

1371. Success Not An Offer

You get on "a platter of gold" cheaply.
You must be ready to walk the crooked roads
That lead to it:
Deceits, disappointments, and criticisms.
At every turn failure which is a good
Companion to the inept and lazy people
Will try to meet and welcome you in its arms.
You must be resolute and uncompromising.

1372. Global Unity

Through inter – tribal,
Continental and religious mixed marriages
Will establish a strong and cohesive bond
Between people of the future world.
We urge religious bodies of whatever calling,
Practitioners of traditions to liberalize
And enhance mixed marriages.
After all you all call on the same creator.

What a better place the world will be
When a man and a woman from any
Remote part of my continent has a brother
And a sister as a native in all the continents
Through mixed marriages
Although the ceremonial grant of citizenship helps
To foster international relationship, the real blood
Relationship will further cement global unity.
We shall then be hoping that the future generations
Shall become one united family.
Presently modern transportation mode
Of travelling and the social media platform
Are doing a lot bringing everybody
Across the globe together in one
Global village.

1373. "Thy Kingdom Come"

Is eager expectation by all religious practitioners.
Meanwhile the sons and daughters of the
So – called Adam and Eve do not want
"Thy will be done" on earth by turning it
To devil's kingdom.
If by their evil activities are blocking
The only passable road how will
The kingdom of heaven pass through
The barriers to come to earth?
The depth of your belief will give you the answer,
Or perhaps the kingdom of heaven
Is only in the mind of individual believer.

1374. The Ordeal Of The Aged

Who has reasons to travel from one place
To another in his country which lacks
Effective means of transportation,

In some places none.
A country which cannot boast of good transport
System but depend solely on motor bikes as
Means of mass transit is a country whose
Peers had left behind.
A country which subjects the elderly,
Women and children to unpleasant experiences
Being the most vulnerable citizens.

1375. An Appendage To Creation

A clearer insight.
To create is to build or mould an object
Or an idea from something already existing.
To emanate is to emerge from the abstract
Or was not previously existing,
Physically that is.
Therefore the dense matter became materialized
Through emanation which gave birth to the universe
And all the hosts.
The dense matter originally emanated from
The Creative Intelligence – Life!
Life is a mystery man will never find its source,
Much less solve it.
All living and non living things evolved from matter.
As earlier explained emanation has no physical
Action you can observe.
So also evolution.
In evolution you cannot observe,
Unlike creation in practical action,
Its progress of action as the object grows.
Unlike emanation things evolve or develop
From something already existing.
Although things can also originate from things
Already existing without physically creating them.

The word emanation can be used to describe them.
For example smoke emanates from a burning wood
Already existing.
Neither the wood nor the fire created it
But their action produces it.
Striking hard objects like iron or stone against
Each other will produce sparks.
The sparks were not created but emanated from the action.
God did not create life.
He is life and all things universally emanated from Him.
Not talking religion Lord Jesus said: "I Am The Life".
The Creative Intelligence In a human body.
The belief was once held that scientist do not
Believe in the existence of God.
I think what they meant was that God
Was not a physical Being but unseen Intelligence.
For instance we do not see the air or breeze
But the particles it carries.
In the same way we cannot see God as Spirit,
We see Him in His creation.
The limited intelligence of man cannot comprehend
The fog of mystery which surrounds life,
Not even science can fully unravel it.

1376. Striking Names

Of those who left their foot – prints on the sand
Of time with noble or ignoble deeds.
The names were not however picked for performances
But names that strike a chord of high sounding
And also are not common.
They however stood out too for the role
They played during their time.
Abraham Lincoln: 16th American president.
Adolf Hitler: His attempts to rule the world

Thereby plunged the world into two world wars.
George Washington: 1st American president after
The independent war for self – determination
From Britain as General Officer Commanding (GOC).
Jesus Christ: The great teacher who came
To sacrifice His life to save humanity.
Joan of Arc: Her exploits in the wars between
Her country France and Great Britain.
Johnson Aguiyi – Ironsi: Nigeria's 1st military head of state.
Julius Caesar: A warlord and ruler of ancient Rome.
Margaret Thatcher: The iron lady and Britain's
1st female prime minister.
Methuselah: Biblical longest living man.
Nimrod: Biblical mighty hunter for the Lord
Who established Babel.
Napoleon Bonaparte: A young gunner whose ambition was
To rise in the army to qualify for a baton
And ended up an emperor of France.
Nebuchadnezzar: The maximum ruler of Babylon now Iraq.
Nnamdi Azikiwe: Political activist who tried
To be a nationalist but was not given a chance.
Nostradamus: Predicted many great events,
Most which came to pass.
Osama Bin Laden: He took on the world
As a terrorist in defense of Islam.
William Shakespeare: The great English poet and playwright.
Wilson Churchill: Britain's prime minister
During the 2nd world war.
Yakubu Gowon: Nigeria's 2nd military head of state
Who fought Nigeria / Biafra civil war.
These are names of great men and women
My limited knowledge could pick.
The underlined are the striking names.

1377. Parental Love,

Reasons why children love their mother than their father.
Though the father's spermatozoa develop
The egg of the mother and also
Determines sex of the child, love for both
Tends to sway to the mother than the father,
Especially the male child.
It will be stupidity for any father to sulk at this.
By virtues of the mother carrying the child
In her womb and on her back,
Sucked the milk of her breasts are strong
Factors that establish strong relationship,
Strong affinity and attachment between child and mother.
As in all things without exception some children,
Especially the females feel strong love
For their father than their mother,
Though negligible in number.

1378. In Coma!

Electricity since the third republic in my country Nigeria
Is at the throes of death,
Suffering from serial epileptic seizure and goes into
Coma every now and then.
The cause of the ailment is diagnosed massive
Theft of its yearly lifeline appropriated billions
On regular bases to give steady and regular
Light to the citizens so they can see
Their way around and carry out their businesses.
As a result of the yearly appropriation and
Misappropriation game of hide and seek
By the mighty lions and lionesses
Light goes into regular off and on blinking.
It can be compared with a patient going
Into reoccurring lapses because the doctors,

Nurses and other medical hands connived
To pilfer money to buy him drugs
For a permanent cure.
When I see light in foreign countries
On the TV screen turn night into day,
Well designed and elegantly equipped train cars
Smoothly gliding on the rails my heart
Bleeds for what is happening to my country.
Why could we not be able to build necessary
Infrastructures when we have better economic
Potentials to do better?
We saw what our late sage did in the old
Western Region and promised to replicate
These good services here.
We refused because we are not patriotic
Enough to serve the country faithfully and make
It good and better place for coming generations.
Our greedy mentality works exactly the same way
Of the rats who will not be so foolish
To put the cat in charge of their grains.
The cat will not eat the grains but will not
Also allow the rats go near them.
This was why the late sage's services were rejected;
He would not permit free looting of the treasury.
At this junction is where we reach the crossroad.
Which right direction do we go?
Rich with mineral deposits of different kinds
And an agrarian country, Nigeria has no excuse
To be poor.
But for mismanagement of her resources
She has all it takes to rival and be the envy of
Other well developed countries.
We have the will and the expertise to do it
And even better.

But our avaricious nature to grab it all
Has continued to block our progress.
Ever heard of Alibaba and the forty thieves?
I have but cannot recollect the story.
I guess Alibaba and the forty thieves had idea
That they had the rights and privileges like
Our lions and lionesses to go thieving
As the lords of the minor.
The problem has always been our self – centered
Mentality to own everything and in excess
To a point of madness.
We use public money to build magnificent mansions
For self and children,
Present and yet unborn.
The remaining we offload into local and foreign banks.
In the midst of all these frauds light suffers serial
Epileptic seizure.
These despicable behaviours prolong the sufferings
Of the common man and his children.
In the end probes are set up by members
Of the inner circle headed by loyalists.
Here the game of hide and seek starts
Only to turn out hunter becoming the hunted.
It is designed to hoodwink us the mere mortals,
Otherwise the reader will want to know why probe
Findings often fail to see the light of the day.

1379. "Slow Men At Work"

Is a warning sign written on a plain plank
Facing the on – coming traffic usually seen
At the sites where men of the Public Works
Department (PWD) of the ministry of works
Are repairing roads.
The warning was meant to draw the attention

Of the drivers to beware of the working men
And drive slowly to avoid causing harms.
Members of the public knew them as slow workers
At duty post.
It is therefore ironical they should confirm this
Lackadaisical attitude to the public through signpost
Designed to warn approaching traffic.
Was it a problem of English or a system of writing?
It should have been written:
"Slow. Men (are) at work". Or "repair work ahead".
Everybody knew the lackluster manner the men
Did their work.
Is Public Works Department in the works ministry
Still in operation today?
If it is do the men still work the same way
As their fathers did before them?
Officially ministries are constitutionally empowered
To serve government and the people.
However the unconstitutional policy of the workers
From the top down to the bottom is not
To work hard and fast.
Ask in any ministry the workers will confirm
The statement through body language.
If they deny and try to cover up the smoke
Oozing out from the chimney anybody can see
What is plain enough to see.

1380. He Started Dancing

When the music was yet to start playing.
Like the fool with a basket full of eggs
In front of him who daydreamed of his
Expired riches.
You know the story but I decided to add it
To my stock of historical philosophies in the

Stable of Timeless Echoes for those who may
Not have read or heard about it before.
The beginning of his growing riches was
When the eggs hatched and the chickens fully grown.
The envisaged growing poultry business soon
Started to yield good returns,
Built a big house and married.
The business grew and expanded with many hands
To manage it.
He added another business which soon became
A conglomerate entity.
He had now achieved the status of a business
Tycoon with a horde of workers and servants.
Any worker or servant who dared to mess up
He would kick…
He swung his foot forward.
The daydreaming dissolved to reality only to find
The floor in front of him messed up with broken
Eggs and an empty basket lay on the floor on its side.
The story of over ambitious fools who count
Their riches before they own them.

1381. Animals Do Not Behave

Based on remembrance.
They have no retentive memories to recall
Past events or behaviours.
They depend largely on instincts in reacting
To situations of the moments.
Hit your domestic animal for whatever reason
It will run away but after a while repeats
The same thing if similar situation presents itself.
Set a trap with a bait for an animal.
If the trap springs but the animal escapes
It will try yet again to snatch the bait when

Next passing by where the trap and bait are.
That the trap had once tried to catch it
Does not register any recollection of it.
Instincts warn them to run or attack
In defense if feel in danger.
While a man is steadily climbing higher
On the intellectual ladder, the animal is still
On the lowest rung and will remain there.
Besides achieving intellectual and technological height,
Man must not leave behind spiritual morality.
It is then he can truly and proudly claim
To be above the level of animal.

1382. Economic Chain

Is non academic exercise but a layman's
Knowledge of how a good government should manage
The resources of a country.
Government is the big spender and all earnings
From various economic sources are remitted
Into the coffer which is the Central Bank,
The custodian of government monies.
Through the Central Bank government controls
All economic transactions through physical policies
With an economic blue print to promote growth
In both public and private sectors.
It controls inflow and outflow of monies
And safety valve to prevent leakages in the system.
Physical policies of growth are the constitutional
Responsibilities of the country's apex bank.
It must be headed by a honest and trustworthy
Technocrat who also must be surrounded by
A team of trustworthy financial experts.
The citizens own both government and the
Public purse which is the Central Bank.

For the country's wealth to go round to the
Grassroots government owes it a duty to pay
Its workers regularly, contractors to government
And other contractual obligations so the economic
Wheels can run smoothly on equally smooth groove.
It is the constitutional responsibility for a good
Government to see to it that the economy performs
Creditably.
Two of the major reasons why government
Is in power in the first place are security
And vibrant economy.
There must be security to life in all sectors,
Buoyant and healthy economy to benefit all.
Badly and poorly managed resources will cause
Economic stagnation in the system.
When government honours all contractual obligations
The wheels of the economy run well to benefit
Everybody.
This is the economic chain through which money
Gets down to the traders, artisans and all others
Who are not on government payroll.
This is an economic chain of activities.
Government must be able to meet its promises,
Alive to its constitutional responsibilities and
Obligations to the people.
Provision of functional and lasting infrastructures
Which are vital components to drive the economy,
They are key to a robust and healthy economy.
Managers of any country know this and the
Right direction to steer the wheel of country's
Economic vehicle.
Instead many of them embark upon dramatized
Jourey of merry – go – round ride which often
Ends with no meaningful outcome.

Such leaders are not leaders in politics
But political leaders purposefully in politics
To feather their own nest.
They are the types of leaders who trigger
Uprising and set in motion the reign
Of anarchy.
The economy must perform well to benefit
Everybody if the managers do not want
The Yoruba proverb to happen which says:
"You do not use the head of a snake to
Scratch the nose".
Fortunately for the leaders in my country
The teeth of the snakes are blunt.

1383. Ooh! Aah!

Is all the response of the world in sympathy
For the death of any person.
No death of a big man or small man
Can scare the world from moving on.
What the big man or small man will earn
After death is ooh! Aah! sympathy.
After that everything dies down and everybody
Goes back to his or her own normal business.
Many people attend the burial of the big man.
They know the bereaved family will entertain
Them with big feast at the after - burial party
And eat to their satisfaction.
Few attend the burial of the small man;
Nobody wants to waste his or her time
Where there will be not much to feast on.
It is a world nobody is ready to die for anybody.
Both big man and small man get final
And equal reward – six feet deep down!

1384. The Possible Meaning

When Jesus the Christ pleaded with God
As Son on the cross: "Father,
Forgive them for they know not what they do".
Those who arrested and crucified Him only
Acted the divine script no power on earth
Could avert.
It was as much as telling the people
They were carrying out His wish.
As mentioned earlier He told Pontius Pilate
This much.
Authority in Rome tried to stop it and failed.
The emissary could not arrive Jerusalem until
Everything was over.

1385. A Battle Of Supremacy

Between satisfaction and greed.
Who wins?
When animal has had its full belly
It let go of the remaining carcass and no longer
Goes after other prey until it is hungry again.
When man has gotten all he wants
He goes on acquiring more than he needs.
Animals feed on the moment of hunger,
Man goes on greedily adding more
And to waste.
Presently greed is winning more grounds
Against satisfaction.
A higher percentage of human beings
Are greedy above the average.

1386. The Circle Of Life

Is a non academic and intellectual knowledge
But a deduction of the writer.

All organic living things breathe in air
That contains oxygen to be able to remain alive.
In turn we breathe out air contaminated carbon
Dioxide which is absorbed by the vegetation as
Its own system of breathing;
In this way it is purified back into oxygen.
This way the circle of life continues to revolve.
Were there no more forests and other greens
To purify the contaminated air we breathe
All organic creatures will die off.

1387. No Record Of First Man

Even after his descendants began to populate the earth.
Who did the recording?
Was it his immediate descendants or the later
Generations who were yet primitively ignorant?
Was it from mouth to mouth story of his emergence?
With the level of awareness would it not be lost
In the gloom of the years gone by?
It would if even they had the sense of it:
Unless we are denying ourselves the truth.
Nobody could give the specific manner through which
Our first ancestors evolved as full human beings.
Once I saw a crude sketch of imaginary images,
Ape – like appearance,
Of our likely ancestors walking in stooping gait
Although unlike the apes without hairy body.
Nobody could give accurate accounts of what were
Not known to anybody.
Otherwise they were imaginary accounts.
The age of the first products of the human
Species went far back beyond the stone age.
It was largely the darkest age enveloped
In a blank sheet of fog science could not penetrate.

The first human beings through evolution,
Even their immediate progeny through birth,
Were ignorantly stone blind and deaf
To elementary knowledge.
They lived a simple life dimly aware of existence
For the sake of living.

1388. You Will Never Die,

A man said to me as a prayer;
Though I regarded it as a curse.
I asked him if he had ever seen anybody
Who had not ever died.
I will not tell you his answer but we will
Work towards it,
Though you might know it already.
Man knows he will die though, when and how
He does not know.
Yet he plans for the future as if he
Will not ever die.
If the animals have the sense to store
Their particular food,
Except a very few of them do,
They do not because they think not of tomorrow.
As far as they are concerned tomorrow
Does not exist.
It is only man by nature plans and saves
For tomorrow to enjoy the fruits of his labour
Even when he does not know if he will
Live till tomorrow.
Does he not have his descendants in mind,
Which animals do not have?
At this stage you still do not get the why?
Of course,
All we have said cannot give you the why.

The man is simply saying I will continue
To live through the generations of my children.

1389. Wrestling

Is an international sport developed through genes
By every race.
Hence every race has its own peculiar way
Of practicing it.
The English has its own modernized practice
By throwing the opponent on the canvas.
If you are able to pin him down on his back
You win after the counts of ten.
The American version is the same except it has
An element of brutality.
In Africa,
With emphasis on my own locality,
You only have to throw your opponent on the ground,
On whichever part of the body he lands,
Fall on him or not you win.
In fact not falling with the opponent is regarded
As an exponent in the game.
Football game originated in England which today
Became a global mother of all sports.
Boxing was not originally a game but a manner
Of fighting also through genetic practice.
It was later modernized as an entertainment sport
Which also gained international recognition second
To football.
I refer to genes because the practices of these games
Were not copied from one race to another.
They were developed through gene by individual race
That practices them hence their global spread.
Initially every race had its own way
Of using boxing to fight an opponent.

Referring once more to my local environment
Boxing was in crude form.
You clench your fists tightly,
Draw backward whichever hand you are using
And swing it forward at your opponent.
No element of protecting any part of the body.
Every race now adopted the modernized method
By raising your fists and arms in front of you,
In the manner of praying mantis,
To be on guard as a protection
Against your face and body,
And also on the ready.
Africa had many indigenous games but we
Did not have the initiative to develop any,
And we could not recognize their social relevance
On human life.

1390. Science Of Preventing

Suspects or prisoner's escape by running away,
Mostly against the blacks,
Is practiced by law enforcers in the United
States Of America.
When caught for an offense or in prison already
The affected persons' belt or anything that holds
The trousers tight to the waist are removed.
The trousers becomes loose and this affects
Hard and fast running.
This is the science in it:
When running you swing your arms for
Free ovement and higher speed.
If you are forced to hold onto your trousers,
The Americans call it pants,
It will slow running and reduce speed.
If you decide not to hold the trousers against

Your waist it will slide down and entangle
Your legs and you fall
Notable freely to swing your both arms
Limits your speed.
For instance place both the fastest runner
And the last to breast the tape for a race.
Tie an arm of the fastest runner to his side
While leaving the slowest runner's arms free.
The slowest runner will breast the tape first
To beat the fastest runner.
The above method to prevent criminals
Running away is what our youths watch
The Negro musicians do on Television.
They are making themselves voluntary criminals.
Not all things you watch on stage are good
Materials for public display.

1391. Danger Of Jealousy

Is when you are using it to spite those
Who had made it a success.
Do not jealous and envy your better neighbour
But aspire and work hard to be like him,
Even endeavour to surpass his achievements.
But avoid over ambition that may cause a blockade
Against your efforts.

1392. "God Is My Witness"

Is a readily oath to swear to clear us
Of misconducts.
We Know God will not physically come
To bear us out or exposes us liars.
Our conducts will stand in place of God
To uphold the truths of our words or expose

Our lies.
We can block the course of human justice,
Purposefully or in error.
Nobody can block the course of natural justice.

1393. "So help Me God!"

The time honoured concluding part of oath
Swearing by accused person in the dock in court.
On what basis?
For telling the truth or lie?
The Holy Book had guaranteed that "the truth
Shall set you free".
Without appeal.
Indeed truth will vindicate you.
As a Yoruba proverb has it:
"If lie is on the run for twenty years
It will take only one day for truth to catch up".

1394. The Old Soldiers

Whose ranks range from septuagenarians to
Centenarians who had been fighting the battle of life
Since youth are in the last trench for the last battle.
The enemy soldiers are senility,
Feebleness and all manner of ailments attacking
The vulnerability of their weak condition.
By the rule of engagement individual must die
On the battle field.
Before then the struggle continues with doggedness.
All hail old soldiers,
It is about obeying the law of growth and decline.
Never say die until six feet under.

1395. Spiritual Body (2),

True or false assumption?

I believe in spiritual or astral body without being
Superstitious as dream and shadow are realities.
As I also said earlier dream is a metaphor
Of spiritual life.
I spoke about spiritual body before.
I am laying emphasis on it that in our dreams
What we carry around is spiritual body which is
Not affected by whatever ailment is assailing
Our material or physical body.
The same reason why aged person is seen
In his or her prime state,
And deformed person without any blemish.
I used moon as an example:

We see the moon in its various shapes
Due to the movements of the earth
Round its Satellites.
Yet the moon remains in its zenith
All the time of appearances, also the sun.
I made reference to pain induced dreams;
In such situation you feel pain.
For examples,
If down with severe malaria it may induce
Hallucinatory dream in which you see some
Unpleasant caricature figures.
If you are about to fall from your bed it
May induce a dream of falling into a gully
Only to wake up and find yourself actually
Fall off your bed.
Of course the spiritual body
Called shadow body in my birth place,
Is not involved in what is happening to your
Physical body.

1396. Nothing Beyond The Power

Of God by all things He created;
Their power stop where His begins.
As a Yoruba proverb puts it:
"God has not created what He cannot subdue".
And He will never do.
All things made by man,
Though serve his purposes,
Fight him back by causing him harms
And deaths.
Nothing he can do about it.
He has to continue making the sacrifices with
His life for their uses since he cannot
Do without them.

1397. The World Coming To An End

Is a religious prediction not backed with scientific facts.
The universe was not put in place in isolation
From its hosts of galaxies,
The planets and satellites.
The earth planet does not exist in isolation
From other planets in our galaxy –
The Milky Way.
Our own galaxy does not exist in isolation
From other galaxies.
All exist and behave in united harmony under
The universal law.
It is a win one wins all affair.
Man only and other organic creatures are
The endangered species through man's
Damaging activities we already warned against.

1398. The Bitter Truths

We must live with as human beings are
The basic things we all need to live happily

But some people are denied of them.
There is nothing humanly possible we can do about it,
An inevitable fallout from the intrigues
Of life.
Nobody is ill-health free:
Some people are prone to chronic health problems,
Terminal or not,
That subject them to pains or inconveniences.
Some men and women will not marry,
Willingly and unwillingly or through circumstances.
Many people will not be able to own houses,
Some not even able to afford rented roofs over
Their heads.
Many people do not have children,
Just single one,
Tried as they can throughout their lives.
So many other people are denied even the simplest
Basic things they need to move on well with life.
All these oddities are the lot of human beings
We must live with in good faith
As a matter of facts.

1399. "Words Spoken By The Babe"

Says the Sage,
Are words from God which must be taken
With seriousness.
If a child warned you on a matter above
His Knowledge you must take them as words
From God and obey.
If you disregard and disobey them
You did not disobey God but your conscience.
It is you who get the punishment of disobedience
Against what you were warned.

1400. Superstition (2)

Has no part to play in our success or failure.
Our belief or non belief on a project,
Or how our life should play out,
Does not influence our success or failure.
It is only a mere superstition or belief.
What will influence our performances to achieve
Good or bad result is seriousness or lack of it
We attached to our efforts.
Superstition is a product of ignorance which was
Given birth to in the dark days.
It has no place in these modern days of civilization.

1401. Government Hired Protesters,

Though not government per se but the officials
Who are elected and appointed to run the business
Of government on behalf of the country and the people.
The first aim is to counter the protest as anti
Government and unpopular by engaging counter
Protesters to fight and disrupt the protest to weaken it.
The second aim is to use the hired protesters
To destroy and loot government properties
To give them opportunities to appropriate money
For repairs and replacements.
It is through this corridor money is appropriated
Into private pockets.
Their political thugs and other miscreants
From the poor segment of the society are
The ready hands for recruitment.
These people know that if the protest against
Government succeeds it will also benefit them.
But loyalty to the political party first and
The measly change to buy them cannabis
Do blind them against better reason.

Officials in the opposition political parties
Also recruit counter protesters to join the anti –
Government protesters.
Of course if they are in government tomorrow
They may do worst.

1402. A Salute To OBJ

For making available the services of Global
System of Mobile (GSM) communication affordable for
Us without costing much on the high side and
Out of the reach of the poor.
It has brought everybody together into one big
Roomy parlour so we can talk,
Transact business and carry out social engagements.
Somebody was digging an insinuation into my left
Ear that after all it was General Sani Abacha who
Started the GSM business before he died.
We know our OBJ had always been a lucky man
Who was always called upon to complete a job
Started by somebody else.
And he always achieved results in doing them.
Whether the jobs were done well or done badly
Is an opinion of individual person.
Where lies the criticisms of who started or
Did not start any job?
Who does not know that in a relay race
The last of the team with the baton to breast
The tape is the star of the victory?
He or she could make or mar the efforts
Of the first threesome.
Simple.

1403. Easy Way To Kill A Country

Is through running down its economy,

The main bakery room where all the bread
And other confectionaries are baked.
This can be through inadequate or non
Availability of functional infrastructures,
Weak and non performing institutions and
Lackadaisical attitude of the civil servants
To their constitutional responsibilities.
To cap it all ineffective policies of government
To prevent a systematic collapse of social order.
All these put together you have a dead country.

1404. Tell Me The Difference

Between Biblical burnt offerings (sacrifices) to God
And traditional sacrifices (offerings) by the priests
To the gods through their divinations.
In the Biblical burnt offerings rams were used
And it was often God Himself who requested
His prophets to build altar and make burnt
Offerings to Him.
Sometimes the prophets on their own volition
Would tell the people to offer burnt offerings
For one reason or another.
The altars were built with dry woods and the
Burnt offering animals were usually rams.
If the smoke went straight skyward it meant
Acceptance by God.
If the smoke spread it was a sign of rejection.
This is how the Bible made us to understand it.
The traditional sacrifices are mainly of two-fold:
Sacrifices to the gods of the community is revealed
Through divinations by the priests and to be
Made at the community shrine.

Domestic animals are usually used for the peace
And prosperity of the community.
A family or an individual might wish to consult
A priest for a child,
Good health and plenty yields or material things.
Through divinations the priest could recommend a sacrifice,
Usually a cock.
The Sacrifice could be made in the community shine
Or in the corner of the room's shrine to the ancestral spirits.
While traditional sacrifices still holds way, the Biblical
Burnt offerings had taken a new dimension since
After the death of Lord Jesus Christ.
Today offerings are made in money or material things
As demanded by the clergy of the church,
And other houses of worship.
Burnt offerings and traditional sacrifices are peculiar
To individual group of people and religious denominations.
They have different ways of observing the rites.
Before the first copy of the Holy Bible came
To Africa, different communities had their ways
Of practicing sacrificial offerings to the gods
Of the land.
If God was said to be demanding for offerings,
For whatever reasons,
Like requesting Abraham to offer his son Isaac
To test his loyalty,
What then are the reasons to brand the traditional
Sacrifices as heathen practices?
Burnt offerings or sacrifices actually signify respect,
Loyalty and recognition for the power to whom
You are making them as owner or controller
Of your destiny and life.
If you follow Bible accounts about God and His
Dealings with man since the Biblical periods

He seemed to have changed a great deal.
I will always believe God is unchanged.
Not even any of the elements He created
Had changed since some billion years of existing.
I have not heard or read from any source,
And also ever heard that anybody else did,
That any of His created elements had changed
Shape or behaviour.
Otherwise we should today be referring to a former
Earth planet as an example.
If there was a change during its pristine period
It was a planet suffering the effects of still in
The process of creating.
Should God change the universe would be plunged
Into a catastrophic upheaval of monumental proportion.
It means God is unchangeable Universal Power.
It is the way we see God and understand Him
Then and now that had changed.

1405. The Immortals of The Earth.

A symbolic citation since it is not possible to mention
All names.
The title quickly suggests to the mind men who
Did not die in this world.
What the subtitle really means are men who had
Immortalized their names in remarkable ways
To earn them everlasting recognition.
Names which are being worshipped and revered
From generation to generation.
Great men who died as mortal beings,
Whose unequal contributions immortalized them
In the memory of the world.
Men who excelled in the fields of science, discovery,
Invention and religion, etc.

Their works and names endure!
To mention names will be an uphill task for this writer.
Their names alone will make a big volume of a book.
The important lesson in this particular subtitle
Has to do with you and I being inspired by it.
Let us emulate their noble examples of sacrificing
Pleasure and life to make the world better
For generations coming after them.
We should contribute our little quota to make
The present ailing material world a conducive
And habitable place for us all.
I can only present very negligible examples:
Braille as a boy went to his father's foundry
Workshop in his absence.
Sparks flew into his eyes and became blind.
Later he invented Braille reading device for the blind.
For a blind it's smacks of a miracle invention.
Jesus Christ of Nazareth on whose name Christianity originated.
Martin Luther - King (Jnr.) of America for his
Non-violent resistance against racial ill-treatment
Of the black race in America.
Michael Faraday who invented electricity.
Prophet Mohammed of Saudi Arabia who founded
Islamic religion.
Stevenson who drew inspiration from a boiling
Kettle to invent steam engine which gave birth
To locomotive engine.
Three merchant sailors William Wilberforce,
Christopher Columbus and Francis Drake (aka Elizabethan seadogs)
Discovered the virgin land of North America.
Wright Brothers of America built the first flying Aeroplane.
The list goes on and on...
You will add those in your mind.

1406. United Nations,

An august body comprising nations from
Both super and underdeveloped countries
To come under one umbrella after the end
Of second world war in 1945.
Since its establishment the organization
Has been doing its best to restore global
Peace in a troubled world.
Its best seems not quite good enough,
The world not devoid of pockets of wars
And other crises here and there.
Most as results of the superpower nations
Flexing their muscles.
I cannot make a good job of this write-up
To replace the missing copy put together under inspiration.
In my first attempt I assigned useful roles
The body must play to save the organic lives
Of the future world gradually becoming the endangered
Species under different indices treated in various
Subtitles and restore global peace.
I raised a salient point in the last copy,
For equity and fairness every continent must
Have at least a seat in the decision making
Organ called Permanent Seat.
It gives sense of belonging and further strengthen
The organization.
Of course the post of Secretary - General is assigned
To non permanent member countries.
What is Secretary - General after all but an errand
Boy except that he or she enjoys publicity gag.
The body must make sure no country
Claiming exclusively ownership rights is allowed
To destroy its major forests in the name of
Development or for other excuses.

The Amazon and other major forests must be
Protected so they continue to provide much needed
Oxygen by all organic creatures to survive.
The forests around the world are a chain
Of protection for cleaner and healthy environment.

1407. Two Alternative Possibilities

Man will never be able to unveil the mystery
Of which either is the true position.
It is either when we die we wake up into
Another life as when we are in dream,
Of course with full awareness of existence
But no recollection of a former life;
Or we remain in oblivion as in a dreamless sleep.
Two alternatives neither any living man shall
Ever know.
Lazarus was dead for four days before
The Lord Jesus restored him back to life.
He had no story to tell us what it was
Like beyond death.
Our woman in the North who was dead and was
In the morgue for four days before she revived
Failed to tell us anything.
If we draw a layman's conclusion from
The two examples the dead remains in oblivion
As in a dreamless sleep.
But then the Lord Jesus' promise of heaven
Nullifies this position.

1408. Have I Done It Before?

Do action and time repeat themselves in reality?
Or just in our minds?
You are doing something and it flashed in your mind
That you have done the same thing before,

The same place and the same time.

Yet you are sure you have not done it before.

Yogi Ramacharaka says (not exact quotation):

Nobody who had done something or had been in

A place would not feel had done it before.

Is it a flash from our former life?

I do not think so,

It is more likely a form of hallucination.

This writer had on several occasions experienced it,

Though never involved a place.

I think it is just an imagination of the mind.

1409. Reincarnation,

True or false belief?

Reincarnation of the soul is believed to be coming

Back into this world after death.

Incarnation is a pious soul who advanced to

The higher plane of existence.

Many people,

Including this writer's belief had been in this

Earth plane before.

People in many communities express their belief

In various ways.

The Yorubas express their belief in the system

Of naming the new born baby as the return

Of their father or mother depending on the sex

Of the baby.

In my place when taking the dead body

To its final resting place they accompany it

With the song: "When will you return from soil".

The people believe death is recycling of life.

Some children are born and after a few days or months of birth die.

They continue to repeat the cycles of birth

And death through the same parents.
The Igbos call them Ogbanje and the Yorubas Abiku.
_In the sixties the Sunday Times featured stories
Of two girls with pictures.
One had two stumps as arms and the other black
As coal.
They were repeatedly born to die children.
By way of stopping their coming back and
To serve as punishment they were amputated
And burnt by their parents respectively before burial.
What I don't get is how reincarnating souls did
Inhabit the bodies which had returned to soil
In whatever form?
Wonders of life are inexplicable.
The story of Corey as a reincarnated boy
Was elaborately and convincingly told in
"Stranger Than Fiction".
A boy was killed by his stepmother in our town.
According to people he was reborn a carbon copy
Of his former self.
They gave him same name he bore in his
Previous life.
He told people that he came back because
Of his mother.
I did not know him at home but we met In Lagos as young men.
I later heard that he had died after
He had raised a family.
The subject of reincarnation is very wide.
I only picked some essential parts which I hope
Will convince and educate the reader.
Reincarnation is as true as birth and death.

1410. "Rome Was Not Built In A Day"

Yes. But the building started with

Purposeful determination.
A city of their dream where all the stakeholders
Built for their future generations.
Those who build their city in their pockets
Cannot build their Rome in a million years,
Talkless of days.

1411. Lord Jesus Christ

Humbled Himself to the lowest level and chose
To die a common criminal.
The greatest sacrifice no mortal man could offer
To undergo.
An unparallel and divine offering.

1412. Suffering Under Religious Hiccups

Is a country being governed on the basis of religion.
It will always be embroiled in religious controversies.
A well governed country must abide by its secularism
And moral ethos so it can enjoy tranquility
And peace.

1413. The World Is Deaf And Blind

Hence it could not hear all the moral exhortations
And see the beauty of nature and appreciate it.
If it is a lie tell me why does it keep
Walking on its crooked and evil ways.

1414. How Did We Arrive Here?

We did not know until we started growing.
Then we began gaining more knowledge as from
A dense haze through a tunnel.
As time rolled by the haze became clearer.
We began to see examples how we too found
Ourselves here.
From the examples of those who were arriving

And departing we knew that was the route
We took to arrive here and to depart.
And that we too will be responsible to bringing
Others through the same route.
This is life recreating itself.

1415. A Hero Was Born

Quietly on 29th May, 2015 and we did not know.
The hero, though had no valid ground to contest victory,
Unlike others who would not want to die
And would not mind putting the lives of innocent people
In danger to hold onto power,
Accepted defeat.
He quietly and gentlemanly handed over power.
Our hero – Dr. Goodluck Ebele Jonathan.

Epilogue

The Yoruba proverb says: "words (of wisdom) cannot be exhausted in the belly of an elder". Where the wisdom of one man ends there the other man's own begins. Nobody has the monopoly of wisdom.

Uncountable words of wisdom had been spoken and uncountable others remain yet unspoken. Say the little you are gifted with so people may benefit from them. Only knowledge can liberate the human mind.

I was not expected to learn how to read and write. Somehow, through some twisted fate, I was able to step under the eaves of educational institution and cross its threshold. But for the death of our most senior brother I would have been a farmer and for my artistry skill at youths a bricklayer. Be that as it may, he was largely instrumental to my going to school and also the architect of my being a dropout.

I became convinced that God intended and inspired me to write the unending story of life for the knowledge of the world. If not my limited knowledge could not have made it possible. Also I sincerely believe God preserves me to fulfill a mission, otherwise I should have been dead through accidents on many occasions. Instead I sustain minor injuries every now and then as sacrifices to ward off major mishaps.

When the Lord wishes He makes the fool speak the words of wisdom that will confound the wise. I am as empty and dumb with no ideas of my own like any ordinary man. But when inspiration has alighted upon me words of wisdom flood my subconscious mind and become like an intellectual genius. I regard myself an illiterate in modern standard. In all my plus eighty years I do not know anywhere other than a few towns in the then Western Region of Nigeria. Yet I have travelled the length and breadth of the world through reading. Read books and you will conquer the world intellectually.

Finally, you have read my big message for the world.

This is my unending story of life, those coming after to pick up from where I stopped.

E. Oruamen.

www.ingramcontent.com/pod-product-compliance
Lightning Source LLC
La Vergne TN
LVHW012045160826
845678LV00014B/2707

* 9 7 9 8 3 5 3 3 7 5 2 6 5 *